Secrets of a Vet Tech: The Guide to Low Cost Pet Care when the Cupboard is Bare

by J.C. Farris

ACKNOWLEDGEMENTS and DEDICATIONS

First, thank you to all the animals who have given me strength and inspiration, and have shown me what unconditional love is. To my parents, Earl and Nancy Farris, who instilled a love of nature in me and helped me believe in myself. To Ellen and Bob Barker, for their help in editing the manuscript and for being like second parents to me. To the Scott County Humane Society of Gate City, VA for all you have done to support me and for allowing me to foster for you. To my many friends who encouraged me to write the book when I wasn't sure I could. And finally, to the veterinarians, technicians, farmers, rescuers, and all who have taught me everything I know. You were great teachers.

INTRODUCTION AND DISCLAIMER

We have all fallen on hard times during our lives. Wondering if we can make it until the next paycheck or if we will ever find a job, is not something any of us look forward to. Unfortunately it happens. It becomes difficult enough to feed ourselves and get medical care. What about our pets? Find them a new home? Take them to the shelter? Have them put to sleep?

This is the decision I was faced with. Its one I don't want you to face alone. I'm going to tell you what I did to supply food, medical care, and all the basic necessities, not only to one pet, but to 25 pets. I combined necessity, self sufficiency, and years of professional pet care experience to make it happen and I have shared all that I learned here.

Here's how my journey began...

Growing up in Appalachia in my generation, there were wonderful examples of self sufficiency. My parents built our home by hand, and our extended family tended our own water supply. My grandfather and his sons built a family reservoir that was fed by a stream that caressed down Walker Mountain. If things broke, it was most often fixed without calling a repairman. Even a family church was built to tend to the spiritual side of life. It was a way of living on Walkers Creek.

As I grew up, I tried not to forget the things I learned. Although I moved away, the spirit of the creek continued to run through me. Relocating to the other side of the country was a huge step, but as often occurs, one finds a reason to return close to home.

And so the reason came to me in Southern California, when America's financial crisis finally found my back yard and threatened the care of my pets. I lost my business, my home, everything. When I found my heart was much bigger than my wallet, I realized that I had to do something.

I had always wanted to have my own animal rescue, and my dream came true in a small way while running my business, Gentle Hands Animal Care and Pet Sitting, through out the Inland Empire area of California. I had developed a wonderful network of people, rescues, vet offices, and friends who helped me place unwanted animals. I tended to take in animals with behavioral and physical problems, and, to be honest, many were not adoptable. I couldn't turn them away. The ones who could be placed in a new home, were adopted. However, those who could not be, stayed with me.

Then the bottom dropped out. Gas prices went to nearly $4.00 per gallon and, in my business, that meant a gasoline bill that could exceed $600 per month. A pet sitting client disappeared for over a month, and I cared for his farm full of animals at my own expense, never to see the money again or be paid for the job. Next, after working months without a day off, I became ill and couldn't drive. It was the perfect storm: an the end to life as I knew it.

Financially, the "easy" thing to do would have been to take the pets I had to the local shelter. But I knew what would happen to them. Several were terrified of people and would have bitten the workers. Others had physical issues that would have meant they would be put to sleep. I couldn't abandon them. I wouldn't abandon them.

It was the call of home. It was time to move from Southern California back to the Appalachian Mountains of Southwest Virginia and Northeast Tennessee. There, the cost of living would be much cheaper, and sweet tea could be enjoyed by the gallon! (How I missed the sweet tea of home!)

Getting twenty-five animals across the United States was indeed a chore. It took planning, hard work, and lots of luck. The weather was perfect: cool, but not too cool. It took five days to get all the dogs, cats, birds, and a guinea pig home. It was April when we arrived.

The new home was wonderful. It was not Walkers Creek, but Church Hill, TN. It was an acre property with a remodeled farm house and best of all, my parents were close by. It had an old shed outside that they had prepared to be a large dog house. They had enclosed it with fencing and built a ramp up to the doggie door, so all the dogs could run from their new yard inside to their beds. We insulated it not long after arriving so the animals would stay warm during the winter months. Winter would be a brand new experience for them!

While still working for a vet, I had purchased as much heart worm preventative, flea prevention, and various medications as I could afford. Yet those supplies only lasted for a time. Then I had to get creative.

I've worked in the animal care world since the mid '90's. I've been an animal cruelty investigator, a veterinary technician, a pet sitter, a rescuer, and a certified euthanasia technician. I've worked in up- scale veterinary clinics, and in humane societies which provided limited vet care to the poor. I've assisted small country veterinarians and specialty veterinarians. I took all this experience and began to research in depth. I studied labels. I watched what was being used by the doctors I assisted. I looked at ingredients and even took continuing veterinary technician courses. I utilized every secret, every nugget of knowledge, everything I had learned behind the scenes. This is my story and the results of all that effort.

I am sure I will be criticized by the people who consider pets "just animals" and those who think you should never treat at home. I have heard it before. I did nothing without great consideration and with desperate concern for my pets. I acknowledged when a situation was beyond my abilities.

It should also be noted that every one of my animals were spayed or neutered. Not only would this prevent further offspring, it would prevent many diseases. One doesn't work in animal shelters and veterinary offices without understanding the importance of preventing unwanted litters.

And for those who ask, why not give up the animals if finances were so bad? The answer is simple. No one wants the rejects, the outcast, the perfectly imperfect. Those for whom I could find homes, I did. These were animals, for the most part, who had been rejected by everyone else. They had health problems and terrible social anxieties. Most were over seven years old. People want young, cute, cuddly, and friendly. So it was live with me, or not live at all. As a euthanasia technician, it had been my job to euthanize old and/or sick animals and animals with behavioral problems. I could not do it anymore, especially to my own animals.

After utilizing the things I have learned, I decided to tell my story. Necessity lead me to return to my roots. My purpose is to offer hope to those who find themselves in situations similar to mine and to remind them of that long forgotten art of self sufficiency.

I never intended to write a book about the absolute best care you can give your pet. That is not what this is about and there are plenty of books detailing that. This is about what I could do when I could not afford the absolute best. Its about using common sense and thinking outside the box when life gives you no other choice.

This book encompasses so much for me. It is an autobiography, an encyclopedia of my pet knowledge, and a commentary on the prejudices of families families who are financially poor, but rich in love.

I am frustrated for those forgotten and judged pet parents who love their pets as much as anybody, but are criticized for not being able to provide certain things because of financial constraints. I am angry when knowledge is held back from them that would allow them to take care of their pets because it might cost the animal care industry money. It saddens me when animals are not vaccinated because we have convinced the world that the only proper vaccination is that one that is given by the hands of a DVM. How many litters of puppies and kittens could we have prevented if we shared with their family that their pet could be altered for less than $75? Instead we make them feel guilty for not paying for often optional (and for them unaffordable) pre-surgical lab testing. Sadly, they walk away believing that they will just have to leave their pet unaltered no matter how good of a pet parent they wanted to be. I am angered when rescue organizations have to euthanize animals because they can't afford the high cost of treatment for something that should not cost so much. If they only knew what was possible, the lives they could save.

I am well aware of "best practices" in veterinary medicine. In a perfect world, every pet undergoing anesthesia would have per surgical lab work. Every pet would get yearly checkups, yearly lab work. Each one would be on heart worm preventative, flea preventative, and the best food money can buy. Every client would be a "good client", meaning a compliant one who does as the doctor suggests. Each sick pet would get the needed x-rays, lab testing, ultrasounds. They could quickly be hooked up on IV fluids, medication on board, all without concern for price. But it is not a perfect world. It just isn't.

Think of how many pets, during this latest economic crisis in America, were surrendered to local shelters because the pet parents believed they couldn't take care of them. The standard for "care" has been so greatly expanded over my lifetime, that few of us could live up to it. I certainly believe our pets deserve every wonderful thing we can give them, but to convince ourselves and each other that we are so substandard that we unnecessarily turn our animals in to shelters out of guilt is uncalled for. We can be good pet parents. We just have to learn to think outside the box.

That's what this book is about. It is part of my story of being a rescuer and a vet tech, and what happened when I started was challenged to continue to provide for my own pets. I do not wish to give medical advice and so must offer this disclaimer:

Any information presented is for general information purposes only. This information is not intended to serve as medical advice. I am not a veterinarian. Please contact your veterinarian and discuss your options for treatment. Use of any of the information I provide here is at the reader's risk. In addition, none of the companies or their products have compensated me in any way for mentioning them. I mentioned them because I used them. There is no other reason.

I do hope that it encourages you to stop feeling helpless and learn how to be proactive in your pet's care. Read labels, learn ingredients, research, and think creatively.

Information on any of the medications I mention throughout the book can be found in the chapter "The Pet Medicine Chest". In addition, in the appendix section, I will provide links that I have used for my own research and reference, so you can do your own.

Use this as a starting point to learning everything you possibly can about the pet in your life. Become an expert. You are your pet's advocate. You are her champion, his voice. Love your pet as much as his/she adores you, and you will never be sorry.

TABLE OF CONTENTS

Acknowledgments and Dedications
Introduction and Disclaimer

1. The Reason I Rescue & Share What I Know............8
2. The #1 Way to Save Tons of Money on Vet Bills.....11
3. A Food Snob Learns the Truth about Pet Food........14
4. The Flea Battle Plan.............22
5. Vaccination Protocol Reconsidered.........28
6. Heart worms and Intestinal Parasites.......33
7. Lab Tests I Could Do at Home.........39
8. The Home Physical Exam......43
9. When an Exam Reveals a Concern: Common Illnesses.....51
10. My Pet Medicine Chest.........71
11. Where To Concentrate Your Vet Dollars......83
12. Aging & Letting Go.......92
13. All the Other Details..........95
14. Small Animals, Pocket Pets, Birds, and Exotics....104
15. And the Work Continues........113

Appendix

CHAPTER 1

THE REASON I RESCUE & SHARE WHAT I KNOW

Growing up in Southwest VA, I had loved animals for as long as I could remember and they were always my best friends. It was during a time when few thought about taking their pets to the vet except in an emergency. Spaying and neutering was rarely considered. In fact, I grew up afraid of the vet as the one in our town did not have a good reputation.

Then one day I watched my dear sweet puppy, Pepper, a little Pekingese mix, choke to death on a small piece of candy she had found in my room. My parents tried everything to save her. They rushed her to the vet as they tried to get the candy out. But she died. I thought it was my fault. It was in my room. It was my piece of candy.

I was a tiny, impressionable child. Life wasn't the same after that.

I went on to have other pets, but would often have nightmares of their deaths. My best buddy, Cuddles, who came along after Pepper, was my best friend and companion from about 10 years old until I was in college. I had many other animals, but he was very special to me. I recall sitting on the patio with him doing homework. Other times I recall crying and asking him what was wrong with me? I didn't seem to fit in anywhere, and I felt sad so often. It was Cuddles, who helped me survive my teen years.

He came with me to live at college after I was married and living in student housing at age 19. He knew no fear. One day, when an emergency helicopter landed in the field behind our house, Cuddles took off and ran the length of a football field and tried to jump in. The co-pilot caught him and gave him back to me with a weird look on his face.

Cuddles' body inevitably aged so much over the years and his heart finally started to weaken. He was diagnosed with congestive heart failure. The vet I took him to, Dr. Lee Pilkington, was such a wonderful man. He wasn't scary, and I learned veterinarians could be kind. He allowed me to volunteer at his clinic, when I had the time between work and classes, to see what I thought of veterinary medicine. I loved it.

Cuddles continued to worsen. He was so swollen from the fluid and no matter how much medication he took, things wouldn't improve. The week I knew his end was close, I begged and pleaded with God to take him on, and not make me decide to put him to sleep. But it was not to be.

The day I took him was one of the worst days of my life. Cuddles was ready. When Dr. Pilkington came in to give him the injection, Cuddles handed him his paw. The kindness of that man continued to be evident as he cried with me. I never in my wildest dreams imaged a doctor who would allow himself to feel the sadness of his clients. Even after Cuddles took his last breath, Dr. Pilkington, who knew I had no place to bury Cuddles, told me of a cremation service. Giving me that option made a big difference in my grieving. I wouldn't have to leave Cuddles behind when I left college. So Cuddles was cremated and I still have his ashes.

For someone who couldn't seem to let people close, losing Cuddles was incredibly difficult. I didn't handle it well, but it showed me how important animals were to me and what I was supposed to be doing. My degree in human psychology was put to the side, and a new adventure began.

Dr. Pilkington had encouraged me to go back to school to be a veterinarian using the many college credits I already had. Life got in the way, however, I began working as a receptionist and assistant in veterinary clinics in New Orleans, LA and later in Johnson City, TN.

Over the next several years, the depression and panic I had suffered as a child intensified to the degree that I was unable to maintain my job or my marriage. I was diagnosed with social agoraphobia with severe panic, often unable to leave the safety of my home, a challenge that I continue to confront daily.

Going out of the house was a terrifying experience. My big goal was to go to Wal-Mart which was only fifteen minutes away. I had no incentive. I would dissociate easily, meaning my world would look to me as if a dream, so driving was not an option. My saving grace was the opportunity to serve as an animal cruelty investigator with a local humane society. When someone said an animal needed me, I was focused on helping the animal and found the will to go. As embarrassing as it was, my mother had to drive. Somehow, I did it and discovered new strengths I did not know I possessed.

Over the years as I was recovering I investigated over a hundred cases a year. I educated those who needed it, and those who were simply cruel, had them arrested, prepared the cases and presented them to the judge. I had a 100 percent conviction rate.

I also developed my own little rescue that focused on small pets like hamsters, ferrets, and guinea pigs, having seen so many of these tiny animals brought to the shelter and not finding a home. While living in California, I continued to rescue and still do. Once it's in your blood, it remains.

I have come to realize that saving the animals is the only way of saving myself. As I have continued to battle with my issues, it is the animals who have kept me going. Ms. Ruby, who is my closest companion now, has been with me through so many difficult times- ending relationships, losing loved ones, cancer surgery and the terrible menopause that came with getting the necessary hysterectomy.

The little rescue I have now, which is simply a foster home for Scott County Humane Society is called T.Paws Rescue and ARFranage. Just opening my home so tiny paws can have a place to stay until they find a "furever" home allows me to do a little something to help. The humane society provides the food and necessities, and I provide the space and love. In about a year, more than 20 animals have found homes simply because they were given a little extra time for people to know they existed. Petfinders.org has been tremendous in connecting the right families with the right dogs. Seeing these animals go from being scared after being lost or abandoned, to joining my pack and learning life is good, to finding their new "furever" family, makes life a little sweeter.

So when people say they are "just animals", I have many reasons to differ. People come and go. Jobs come and go. Success comes and goes. But in the end, it is your dog, your cat, your furry or feathered companion, that remains. They open your heart in ways no one else can. And for them, I write this.

CHAPTER 2

THE #1 WAY TO SAVE TONS OF MONEY ON VET BILLS

Sometimes you have to spend a little money to save a lot. Hundreds, even thousands, of dollars can be saved by doing one thing.....spaying or neutering your dog or cat. Before you skip this chapter, give me a chance to explain and I think you will see my point.

As I said, I spay and neuter all my animals. Working in and around the shelters, you know all too well that about 4 MILLION dogs and cats are euthanized every year because of pet overpopulation. However, being a vet tech, you see the physical and financial results of not altering (spaying or neutering).

For instance, it never seems to fail that at some point in the life of an unaltered female dog, she will come into the clinic terribly ill. Often she is running a fever. Her white blood cell count will be sky high indicating a heavy infection. Pyometra will be her diagnosis. "Pyo" as we call it, is an infection of the uterus. The cure? Spaying her. Only this time it won't be cheap. I have assisted in a lot of "pyo" surgeries and it is amazing what we will find. Sometimes, the uterus and all surrounding tissues will be swollen to the size of full term pregnancy, but instead of puppies, it will be full of infection. If not very carefully removed, you can puncture the tissue sending infection throughout the body. The female dog will have to be on IV fluids and strong antibiotics. The incision will probably be much bigger than it would have if her organs had been a normal size. The cost of a surgery like this? Depending on the clinic and the severity of the infection $350-$2500. The cost to have spayed her in the beginning $60-$250.

Before I go any further in explaining how much money you can save by having your pet altered, let me explain a little about the different approaches to spay/neuter and how the cost is affected. I have worked in spay/neuter clinics where the cost of a cat neuter was $21. I've also worked in a nationally known pet hospital where the cost of a cat neuter was $199.

What's the difference? In a spay/neuter clinic where we charged $21 for a cat neuter, the vet's focus is on those two surgeries. Spaying and neutering. He or she is an expert at it. A good vet can neuter a cat in about five minutes. In the one where I worked in California, one technician sedated the pet and prepared the surgical site. The cat was moved to the surgery room and a new surgery pack opened which only consisted of a new surgery blade and new gloves. Since the surgery was so quick, no intubation was required and no gas anesthesia was used. The cat was hooked up to a pulse oximeter to make sure all was well during surgery. The vet neutered the cat (in five minutes or less), the recovery tech took the cat, cleaned the incision site, and stayed with the animal while he woke up. In all the time I worked there, I don't recall losing a single animal.

Now contrast that to my experience as a technician assisting with the $199 surgery at the nationally recognized clinic. When the cat came in, blood was drawn for lab work. The lab work was done in house and takes about 20 minutes or more. This told the doctor if the cat is healthy enough for surgery. While waiting for the lab work to complete, the cat was weighed and the I (the technician) did the math using formulas supplied, so the doctor would know how much sedative to use, and the amount of emergency medication needed should that pet have problems under sedation. Next, an IV catheter was placed in the cat. After the vet reviewed my calculations, a pre-sedative was given to the cat. Once the cat was groggy, he was given an IV sedative and intubated with a tube to allow him to be hooked up to sevoflurane gas. Finally on the table, the cat was hooked up to gas anesthesia and the incision site was prepared. The cat was also hooked up to a pulse oximeter, blood pressure cuff, and ECG machine. Normally, the vet had the surgery done in about five to seven minutes.

The importance of explaining this is to show you that there are options. I felt so bad for the people who wanted to get their pet spayed or neutered yet when they heard $199 and up, they walked away feeling like bad pet parents. More often than not, I caught up to them when no one was looking and gave them information on local spay/neuter clinics.

I'm not saying the medical practice of the procedures in the more expensive surgery is not great. It's probably what vet medicine would be like in a perfect world. But in my opinion, trying to have perfection in a world where 4 million pets a year die because their parents were not spayed/neutered, is irresponsible. I'm sure there is a veterinary practice for everyone. Many people would prefer the comfort of knowing an IV is going into their pet for a surgery that takes five minutes in case something happens. So for them, that is available.

So examine your options when you decide to spay or neuter. Call your local humane society which can point you in the right direction. In our area, as I write this, our local clinic, The Margaret B. Mitchell Spay and Neuter Clinic, in Bristol, VA spays and neuters all dogs for $60, female cats for $55, and male cats for only $40. There is also assistance available to help pay for the surgeries. In our area, it is the Holly Help Spay/Neuter Fund.

Now back to how much money you can save by altering your dog or cats. Many things change when a pet is altered. For the ladies, the risk of uterine and ovarian cancer, as well as pyometra is eliminated. If spayed before the first heat cycle, her chances of breast cancer are drastically reduced. (And if you think breast cancer is rare in female dogs, I can promise you it is not). It also eliminated the chances of venereal tumors. Compare that to the cost of the surgeries, medications, and chemotherapy needed to treat those conditions and you are talking about thousands of dollars. Not to mention that by spaying her, her lifespan and quality of life is much improved.

For the males, at least eight diseases or conditions are either eliminated or the chances greatly reduced by neutering. Those include testicular cancer and torsion (twisting of the testicles), rectal cancer, prostate abscess, cancer, and/or enlargement, hernias, benign perineal tumors, orchitis (infection of the testicles, and venereal tumors (dogs can and do have venereal diseases). Imagine the money needed to treat any one of those diseases.

This doesn't even include the practical side of the issue. Intact dogs and cats have as strong of a desire to mate as the average human male teenager. (Scary, I know). The male of the species (canine and feline) can smell out a female in heat from over a mile away. That's why 80% of the pets hit by car are intact (unneutered) males. They have one thing on their mind and watching for traffic is not it. (Guess how many hundreds of dollars it costs to repair a pet that has been hit by a car? Guess how many don't make it?)

The females also often try to escape and/or drive you insane. I had the unpleasant experience of having a cat, named Chloe, go in heat many years ago. Her spay surgery was delayed because she had needed a bone surgery and needed to recover. At the time, I had lots of small little rescues including a ferret and even a fighting rooster who I had taken as a little guy from an abusive situation. She begged everyone including the rooster to do something. Anything! Nature was telling her she needed to breed! She didn't care with whom or what! Needless to say, the moment the doctor said she was ready for her spay surgery, I had her at the clinic to the relief of the animals at home.

Female dogs, unlike cats, bleed during their heat cycle. That means on the carpet, the furniture, the bed, or on YOU. I am amazed at how many people will buy diapers to put on the females instead of spaying them. It is a waste of money and effort. Dealing with her mood swings are also unpleasant and can lead to aggressive behavior.

Unaltered males tend to fight more and urine mark more often. The cost of having your own dog or cat repaired is one thing. Having an aggressive pet, may mean paying to have the neighbor's pet (or child) repaired. Unaltered male cats tend to pick up deadly diseases and get bite abscesses more often.

Contrary to popular belief, an unneutered male dog is NOT a better protection dog than a neutered dog. And a final note. I realize some men have trouble neutering their male dogs. They feel as if they are doing a disservice to them. In fact, the opposite is true. A dog that does not have to worry about nature's urges can focus on the job at hand. You are helping him live a longer, happier life. If you could give him many more years with you, wouldn't you do it? You can! Don't let your feelings get in the way of doing what is right for your dog. He will not miss out on “the joy of sex”. He will have a greater chance of missing out on the joy of being hit by a car, however. Isn't that more important?

CHAPTER 3

A FOOD SNOB LEARNS THE TRUTH ABOUT PET FOOD

Pet food. What an issue. We have been taught that the amount we spend on pet food equals the love we have for our fur-kids. I bought into it. Years as a vet tech and pet sitter had engrained in me that pet foods available in the grocery store were not good enough for my pets. In California, I spent an untold amount of money having premium dog and cat food delivered to my house so my animals could have the best in the world. I was a food snob.

When I found us in East Tennessee, barely able to buy ANY dog food, I felt terrible guilt buying Purina Dog Chow and Cat Chow, or worst yet, Ol' Roy Dog and Special Kitty Cat Food. I remember one day being in tears over the guilt of not being able to give the best to my fur-kids.

It was crazy to put such guilt on myself. My animals were the happiest they had ever been. They were outside playing in the temperate climate, with an old shed for shelter, with plenty to eat. I had nothing to feel guilty about. We were a family and we were together. That's all that mattered.

Growing up, I don't even recall buying much dog food. The beagle/shepherd mix dog I had as a kid who showed up at my house one day and adopted me, hunted in the woods of Southwest Virginia. Bear, as I named her, was never confined to our property. We lived in a valley called Walkers Creek, surrounded by mountains and family, and no one even considered that pets should be on leashes. So when Bear wasn't hunting for rabbits, she wondered from house to house where she ate the scraps that had been dumped by the creek. She lived a long happy life. I don't recall that she was ever sick until the day she passed away.

Times had changed and so had the world. I knew that I must obey leash laws of course and that my pets would do better being on a steady diet. Human food can cause lots of tummy problems in pets and it is not nutritionally complete. Bear lived a life where she could follow her instincts and hunt for what her body needed. The pets of today do not have that option for the most part.

So I did research. You would never know how controversial the topic of pet food is until you start looking for answers. I couldn't even find consensus on whether dogs are carnivores (strictly meat eaters) or omnivores (both meat and vegetable eater).

The trick to researching on the internet is to find out who is sponsoring the study. Facts and figures can be construed to prove anything. I decided to start at the beginning and study the evolutionary basis of dog and cat nutrition. An in depth article can be found in the Journal of Nutrition. (http://jn.nutrition.org/content/136/7/1927S.long)

The consensus was that although both canine and felines originated in the group of carnivores, they were of different branches. Within the dog family (Canidae), there were carnivore and opportunistic omnivores. Meaning, you eat what you can find, keeping in mind that within the digestive system of prey, you often find grains and vegetable matter. As the canine became domesticated (long before the cat), the body evolved as it relied more on what it shared and could hunt among humans.

Felines, on the other hand, were domesticated more recently. Unlike most domesticated dogs, the cat still retains the instinct to hunt. The nutritional requirements of the cat have not evolved as the dog has, and it is narrower. Cats need more meat than the dog. They also need more frequent feedings (although in tiny amounts) while dogs are satisfied eating once daily.

With these things in mind, there is so much debate as to what is “best” for the pet. Some say a raw food diet. Others say high priced organic foods. Considering my perspective is one of a person doing the best possible thing I can, I continued searching.

A friend suggested checking “Consumer Reports”, a non-biased group that reviews everything from pet food to cars.

What I found was astonishing.

"There's no scientific evidence that any food is better than the next," says Joseph Wakshlag, D.V.M., Ph.D., an assistant professor of clinical nutrition at the Cornell University College of Veterinary Medicine. Pets can thrive on inexpensive food or become ill from pricey food. If your animal is active and healthy, the food is doing its job. A higher price could mean better ingredients and better quality control during and after manufacturing. But you might also be paying for pretty packaging, marketing, or a fancy name.”

(www.consumerreports.org/cro/magazine-archive/march-2009/money/pet-food/overview/pet-food-ov.htm)

In all my research, the only issue I found among all the complaints that seemed to have merit was that certain ingredients can cause allergic reactions in some pets. The first ingredient to be concerned about was the dyes used to make pet food seem “tastier”. It is a human doing the purchasing, and if it looks tasty to us, it must be good for the pet. These dyes have also been linked to some diseases although the FDA disputes it.

(http://www.feingold.org/Research/dyesinfood.html)

What I knew for sure in my experience as a pet parent and a vet tech was that certain foods DID cause itchiness in dogs in particular. So I decided to try to avoid foods that contained Red #40, Yellow #5, and Blue #2 or choose one with less.

As Dr. Wakshlag said, "if your animal is active and healthy, the food is doing its job". (Italics mine). There are some pets who have terrible allergies to certain things in pet food and so a typical food will cause more harm than good. It can cause terrible itchiness, hair loss, and more. I experienced this first hand in my own dogs and chronicle it later.

FEEDING THE DOGS

There is one thing knowing what is best, and another accepting what you can do. I dare say if pet parents were told their dogs needed to consume gold, if they could afford it, their dogs would eat gold. However, the entire purpose of writing this book is for those of us who have found ourselves in a less than ideal situation.

When I first got to Tennessee, I started off with using Purina Dog Chow. The dogs liked the taste, it was affordable, and most of the dogs had little problems with it.

Two of my dogs, Blue and Teddy, did start to have some issues. Blue became itchy and lost a bit of fur. Teddy constantly had loose stool. I decided if the food was the issue, it would be much cheaper and better for the dogs if a food change would solve the problem.

"If it ain't broke, don't fix it" was my motto with the other guys. They seemed perfectly satisfied with their food. I normally buy low sodium chicken broth and dilute it with warm water to pour over their food. Adding the water would allow a small can to go a long way and not add so much as to upset their stomach. I later learned I could buy bouillon cubes even cheaper and make my own broth. More about food additives later.

I knew that it was not only dyes that could be causing problems for Blue and Teddy. Sometimes dogs are allergic to the corn in common dog foods and even the type of meat used. So, to make matters simple, I looked for a food to eliminate both. What I found was Iams Simple and Natural Salmon and Rice. It wasn't a cheap food. Around $18 for a mid-size bag. However, if I was only feeding Blue and Teddy and was measuring the food correctly, I could make that bag last a very long time.

Any time anyone is having skin or tummy problems with their dogs, I already recommend trying a fish and rice based diet. Another item which is great to add to your dog's food is essential fatty acids. This provides something the skin desperately needs. Most EFA products sold for dogs is around $20 for a small amount. Buy it at Tractor Supply in a product for horses and dogs called CocoSoya, and get one gallon for the same price.

I've always made sure to measure the food I gave my dogs. One advantage is saving money. The other is preventing my dogs from gaining too much weight. Knowing that prevention is worth a pound of cure, experience taught me that a fat dog is just asking for problems. No better way to ensure vet bills than to allow your pet to be obese. So free feeding was NOT an option for my pack.

Another way to keep them healthy and their weight appropriate is to supplement part of their diet with items such as green beans and carrots. My mother often canned her own green beans, and so I often shared some of that with them. When that was not available I would sometimes purchase frozen green beans and thaw them.

One of my dogs' very favorite treats is raw carrots. They grab them and put them between their paws like a big dog bone. Be sure not to give too many as they are higher in sugar.

Some people believe that the best food for your dog is a home cooked one. While my dog Bear ate what we (and the neighbors) ate growing up, she also hunted and was able to fill in the "nutrition blanks", as it were. To make a balanced diet for a dog is not easy and it is not necessarily cheap. It's not a simple rice and boiled chicken mixture you can throw together in twenty minutes. You have to consider percentages of meat, carbohydrates, fats, and more.

The complaint a lot of people have with commercial dog foods is the high carbohydrate levels. While I can understand this, I think a better solution to trying to feed a hopefully balanced home-made diet, is adding low fat meat to the bowl and a little less kibble. One has to be careful doing this to avoid intestinal problems. My dogs are used to sharing some of my leftovers in their food. I am careful to avoid foods that can cause problems. Usually, it is just enough to flavor it. I also keep the oil from the foods I fry and add small amounts over several days. Since I feed about 10 dogs at a time (depending on how many are being fostered), I make a large bowl of food, mix the broth or leftovers, some warm water, then divide the food in bowls proportionate to their size. I feed everyone in their crates and watch everyone eat to be sure they are all feeling well.

Below is a list of items that can be toxic to dogs (and cats). Use common sense. A hundred pound dog eats a Hershey's Kiss ®, he will probably be okay, but a one pound yorkie pup eats it, call the vet.

THINGS TOXIC TO DOGS:

- Chocolate – bakers chocolate is the most toxic; can cause seizures and death
- Caffeine products like coffee/tea – similar effect as chocolate
- Grapes and Raisins - cause liver damage
- Macadamia Nuts and Walnuts- can cause weakness, paralysis, avoid nuts in general, but

it seems that occasional peanut butter is okay

- Onions and Onion Powders – destroy red blood cells causing anemia
- Xylitol- a sweetener in many chewing gums and other products, can cause liver failure
- Pits of Fruits such as peaches, cherries, and apples- contains cyanide; rest of the fruit okay
- Tomato plant and/or green tomatoes – can cause heart issues (member of nightshade family)
- Avocados/guacamole -can cause breathing difficulty and fluid accumulation
- Alcohol – causes liver damage, but is much more toxic in dogs than in humans because they are much smaller
- Fatty meats- meats in very limited amounts are okay, but there is a reason the rates of pancreatitis (which causes vomiting/diarrhea) increase at Thanksgiving when a turkey is on the table. MODERATION IS THE KEY
- Coins – if the coin passes within a day or two, damage may not occur, however, I was one of the nurses for a one year old Shih-Tzu who had swallowed a penny at some point months prior and nearly died from zinc toxicity.
- Yeast dough- especially bad for dogs prone to bloat as it can expand in the stomach and cause torsion
- Mushrooms – safely assume most of the mushrooms in your yard are poisonous and get rid of them
- All human pain killers including ibuprofen, naproxen, and acetaminophen. Aspirin is okay under certain conditions and will be discussed later.

Keep this number: ASPCA Animal Poison Control Center — (888) 426-4435 — in a prominent location.

FEEDING THE CATS

So what about the cats? Now that they were outside I wanted to be sure everyone checked in at least once daily and I knew they were eating well. Our property had tons of places to sleep and hide and the cats made the most of it.

My father had been kind enough to enclose a concrete slab that had apparently been intended to serve as a patio. He made the cats a room of their own that was insulated and warm. So it became "Kitty Grand Central" where we all met once daily.

As I have mentioned, there is a lot of controversy surrounding pet foods. With cats it is even more profound because the dietary needs of the cat are narrower. They require a high percentage of meat and less carbohydrate. Some veterinarians are convinced that feeding dry cat food is the cause of many of the ills of the modern day cat because of the high amounts of carbohydrates, grains, and vegetables in them. While the argument is a very good one considering the strong carnivore nature of cats, (In particular I mention the book Your Cat: Simple New Secrets to a Longer, Stronger Life by Elizabeth M Hodgkins DVM), I had to ask myself, if this is so, why do cats who eat dry cat food often live to 15-20 years old?

A little further research revealed a good answer. According to Dr. Elizabeth Colleran, President of the American Association of Feline Practitioners (AAFP) "carbohydrates aren't inherently bad for cats. Rather, cats are just able to derive more energy from protein and use it more."

(http://animal.discovery.com/healthy-pets/cat-health-101/5-human-foods-cats-can-eat.html)

So contrary to what I had been reading, I was NOT killing my cats with dry cat food.

When I look at the available cat food, almost all the foods, dry and canned, inexpensive and expensive have grains and/or vegetables included. The only exception being EVO, from Natura, the makers of Innova brand foods. (12 cans of EVO cat food runs about $20). Blue (R) and Blue Wilderness also sells some grain free foods. (11 lb. bag costs about $36, and one small can of food cost about $1.30).

I spent hours comparing cat foods using a well-known nutrition comparison site called "Binky's page" (http://binkyspage.tripod.com/dryfood.html). What I was looking for was a reasonably priced food that was higher in protein and lower in carbohydrates. I wanted it to have meat as its first ingredient. Know what I found? Not one food that was even anywhere close to my budget.

So the next possibility I inquired into, was canned cat food. That was more reasonable. High protein, lower carbohydrates. Even Friskies ® brand that I had always bought provided a good protein/carbohydrate ratio.

I decided to simply buy the best possible dry food I could, and supplement with canned food. I found I could even cook some eggs for my cats and give them some of the same meat I was eating including boiled chicken and fish.

With all that information in tow after days of research, I decided to step off the guilt train. I loved my cats and was taking good care of them.

The cats were very good about limiting their food intake and getting proper exercise especially now that they were outside. Keeping this in mind, I did chose to free feed them as most cats nibble their food several times a day. Their favorite dry food was either Purina Cat Chow ®, or Friskies Seafood Sensations®. I shared a can of Friskies ® canned food between them to make sure everyone was eating properly.

Some of my friends were awesome and sent me coupons out of their local papers. Another friend taught me to log onto Ebay where I could "buy" coupons for pet food. (The sale of coupons is illegal, so I paid the individual for the service of cutting them out.) Usually, for about a dollar, I could purchase a stack of about 10-20 coupons for a particular cat food. The most common ones were Meow Mix and Friskies.

The one thing that worried me about using these foods was the pH of my cats' urine. Sounds funny, but is super important in keeping your cats healthy and avoiding vet bills. Male cats in particular are prone to urinary blockage. A blocked cat is a dead cat usually within 24-48 hours if not treated. When I could afford it, I kept all my cats on foods such as Purina One ® Urinary Tract Formula. Now I found I couldn't afford that.

I found that I could purchase a tub of potassium citrate with cranberry for about $12-15. I could add it to their food as well as to the dog food if I chose. Both of these have been shown to change the pH in the bladder preventing infections and calcium oxalate stones, which are typical for causing blockages in the first place.

There are some veterinarians who believe the best diet for your cat is home made. However, if you think that getting the ratio correct for dogs is difficult, it is even more so with cats. Most people who make their own home made cat food purchase very expensive meat grinders and many supplements. It is not inexpensive or easy to do. Never attempt it without talking to a vet who makes his/her own cat food. It is not something veterinarians are trained for on a regular basis.

Most of the things that are toxic to dogs are also toxic to cats. There are some items in addition that you should avoid giving your cats. Although some are okay in moderation, it can cause problems and should be avoided.

THINGS NOT TO GIVE YOUR CATS

- Milk- Most cats are lactose intolerant. It can cause major stomach upset. Cat milk from the pet store is an occasional okay treat.
- Tuna- although put in some cat foods, giving straight canned tuna on a regular basis can lead to yellow fat disease (steatitis)
- Liver- again in moderation as too much can lead to Vitamin A toxiosis.

And important note regarding cats and their eating habits is make sure they are eating. When a cat's body gets in starvation mode (for whatever reason), fat starts accumulating in the liver. As it does, the ability of the liver to function is severely impaired. You might notice the whites of the eyes and other mucous membranes turning yellow in color. This is called fatty liver disease or hepatic lipadosis and it is an absolute emergency.

I have to be honest in my personal experience with this. I am embarrassed to admit it, but I feel it is necessary to show what can happen.

At the time I was working several jobs and had several rescue cats. Biskit was a brown tabby who was found in the parking lot of one of my places of employment.

Being so busy, I did not notice that Biskit, was not eating well. In a few days, I finally noticed that she did not look normal. She appeared dehydrated and her color was yellow. I was scared and very angry at myself for allowing this to happen.

She had to go to a specialty vet in Temecula, CA to have a tube passed through her neck, into her esophagus and to her stomach. It was the only way to save her. For 2 months, every 4-6 hours, I, or a family member, would pass watered-down and warmed Hill Prescription A/D canned food through that tube. That continued until she was eating regularly on her own. Not only did she nearly die, it cost about $2000 to save her.

That experience stressed the importance of paying close attention and knowing my animal. If I would have been paying closer attention, I could have prevented a lot of pain for her, frustration at myself, and saved thousands of dollars.

That is why close observation is one of the main tools in saving money as well as the health and life of your pet.

CHAPTER 4

THE FLEA BATTLE PLAN

The animals and I made our way back to TN in April of my 37th year of living. The flea season hit within a month of our arrival. It went from bad to worse. All heck broke loose.

Every one of my animals had been treated with Fipronil (found in Frontline® Top Spot and its generic equivalent PetArmor®) before we even stepped foot or paw onto the property. What we didn't know was that there had been animals at the house previously. A few fleas left behind turned into a population explosion!!

Just one bite from a flea can cause itching enough to drive a pet bonkers. And considering it only takes 10 female fleas one month to produce over 200,000 fleas, and you only see only a tiny percentage on your pets with the rest being in the environment, I knew this wasn't a battle to be taken lightly.

So I instituted a tried and true battle plan and put it into action. The battle was on!!

The Flea Battle Plan:

- Remove the pets from the house and treat the inside
- While the pets are outside, treat the pet
- Move the pets inside, and treat the outer environment

There are a few mistakes people make when it comes to fleas. One is ignoring the environment and only treating the pet. The fleas only die when they bite the treated pet, and they only bite the pet when they need to feed. They can still make them terribly itchy by walking all through their fur. You can use all the products in the world on the pet, but if there are fleas in the environment, they will manage to get on your pet. So many people blame the product. When asked if they treated the environment, most answer "no". If there is one thing I have learned in nearly 20 years of pet care, it is that no step in the flea battle plan can be ignored.

The other mistake so commonly made is convincing yourself that your pet has no fleas. If your pet is scratching him or herself silly just above the tail, your pet has fleas. It is the classic place for irritated flea bites. As I have said, it can take one bite to cause an allergic reaction to fleas. When I see my dogs showing special attention to this area, I check for two things: full anal glands and fleas. Remember, that the life cycle of a flea requires that it only be on your pet long enough to eat a blood meal. While some fleas seem to like to hang out in the fur, others want to jump off and continue life in your house or yard. So look for the evidence of the flea, not just the flea itself.

So, everyone would be moved out of the house, and the house flea "bombed" using an insect fogger such as Raid® Flea Killer Plus Fogger . In my experience, the foggers simply work better than any other product for indoors. I did make sure that all my food was covered and I followed all the directions on the product.

FIPRONIL TRICKS OF THE TRADE

Next, I needed to treat all the animals before putting them back inside. The secret with Fipronil or any other type of topical flea treatment is the oilier the pet's skin is, the better it works. Since it is dispersed along the skin through the oil and oil glands, it is best to apply to a dog who has not been bathed within 48 hours and also one who is dry. Applying it just after a bath is another big and common mistake.

I had learned a smart way to use Fipronil since it was unique. Unlike most other kinds of flea preventative, it was the same medication for dogs and cats, just packaged differently. In other words, the cat application was the same as the dog application, only a different measurement. There is a very slight difference in concentration between dog and cat, in the Fipronil Plus products (which contains Fipronil and methoprene), so I always used the Fipronil only product when using the method described below.

NEVER do this with Advantage® , Hartz® , or any other flea preventative.

However, with Fipronil, I had treated dogs, cats, guinea pigs, rabbits, ferrets, and more over the years. I liked it because it was safer than any other. I had never had an animal get sick from using this product.

Normally, I would purchase a 3 pack of Fipronil Extra Large Dog (89 lbs. and up). The price would vary depending on where it was purchased, but I could count on about $10 or less per vial ($30 or less per box). I opened all the vials at once and put them in a container such as a plastic squeeze bottle. It was important that the container seal properly to avoid evaporation. (Examples of a great container is in the pet medicine chest chapter).

To give you an idea of the savings, ONE $10 vial of fipronil could treat 7 cats or 5 small dogs.

Using a 1cc tuberculin syringe (NOT an insulin syringe), for the smaller doses and a 3 cc for the larger, I dosed my animals accordingly using the chart on the following page.

FIPRONIL DOSAGE

All cats	0.5 ml
Guinea pig	0.1 ml
Dogs:	
0-22 lbs.	0.7 ml
23-44lbs	1.35 ml
45-88lbs	2.68 ml
>89 lbs.	4.0 ml

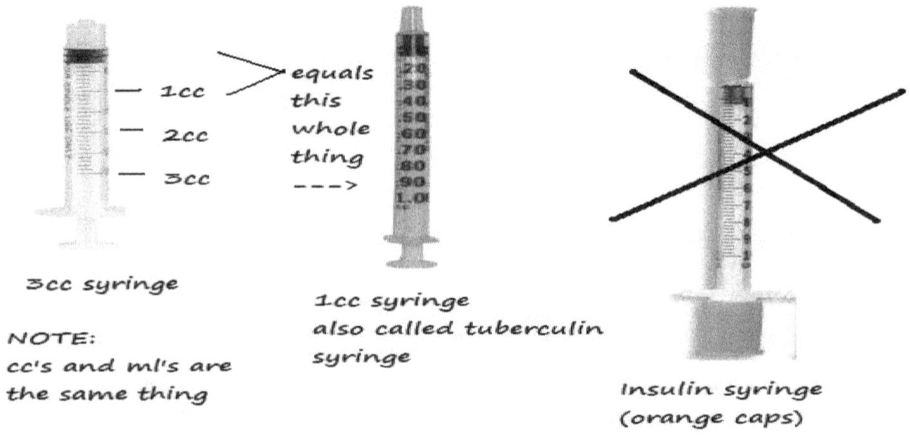

I then treated the yard with a Bio Spot Yard and Garden Spray after moving the animals back inside. It worked and the flea problem was solved!!!!! At least for a while.

DIATOMACEOUS EARTH

Fipronil works for about thirty days. Once it was exhausted and further financial problems made even this difficult to afford, I searched for another solution.

One day while discussing my frustration with inexpensive ways to deal with the flea issue on a social networking site, a friend told me about a natural product she used called Diatomaceous Earth (DE). I was hesitant because I had tried all the natural home remedies before and nothing worked, but it was certainly worth researching.

What I found was pretty interesting. DE is actually a sedimentary rock that is fossilized remains of diatoms, hard shelled algae. It is crumbled into white powder and is sold as either pool grade DE or food grade DE. The difference between the two is very significant. Food grade DE must not contain more than 10mg/kg of arsenic and no more than 10mg/kg of lead. It also contains less than 1% crystalline silica.

I found it is often mixed in with animal food as a dewormer and is even safe for humans to consume.

But how did it kill fleas? Apparently, it dries out the waxy outer layer (called the exoskeleton) of the flea causing the flea to dehydrate and eventually die.

So I talked to more people about it, many who applied it directly to their pet with good results. The three warnings they gave me was to make SURE I was using FOOD GRADE DE, use a mask when applying , and keep in mind it can cause the skin of my pet to dry out if used too often.

It was easy to find pool grade DE, but I had to search hard for the food grade kind. Online I found a product called Thomas Labs D-Flea kit. It was DE powder with a mask and flea comb. The cost was only $30, but I was not ready to order online yet.

Finally, while shopping at my local Tractor Supply, I found it, of all places, in the chicken aisle! It was only $8.99 for 4 lbs. or over in the livestock area for $12.99 for 20 lbs.

I had learned that it was best to wait for a day without rain. Water can make DE completely ineffective. So the next sunny day, the flea battle was on!!!

By this time, the weather was warm and all the animals had been moved outside for the summer. I made sure the yard was freshly mowed so didn't have to compete with heavy grass. I sprinkled the DE on all the dogs' bedding, in their large outbuilding, all their dog houses, in the grass and dirt of the dog run, and on the dogs. I also put it on all the flooring in the outbuilding we had built for the cats, and what was left I sprinkled around the areas the cats populated the most.

Then I waited. A few days later, I bathed the dogs to look for fleas and to remove the DE in case it did dry out their coats. What I found was remarkable. No fleas. I swept up the remaining DE to the corners of the buildings and went on with life happy my friend had been right.

During the next month, I found one flea among our furry population. I didn't want to over use the product because I knew that the DE could also kill any insect with an exoskeleton, some which could be beneficial. If I saw my animals start to scratch, I retreated, including washing their beds, and retreating the yard. If I applied it to the dogs, I always bathed them within 24 hours, and kept close watch on their eyes and nose for any irritation.

It was safe to put on my cats, but not always easy. What I discovered was, that if I put it in their sunny spaces (they loved a sunny drive way), they laid on it, rolled around in it, and covered themselves!

I was thrilled that I could prevent my animals from being tortured by fleas for so little. $8.99-$12.99 for double digit animals compared to hundreds of dollars?

Over the summer, I did notice some outbreaks of fleas. I had to keep in mind that I had outdoor cats who could bring the fleas home. Another issue I had was the drying effect it had on the skin and coats of the dogs as well as irritation to their eyes. I found bathing them within 24 hours was essential. Another good practice was rinsing their eyes out with eye wash after use.

It was working great. Until, the rains came. We had an unusually wet season. DE does not work on wet grass. So, I had to find another solution. Beneficial nematodes.

NEMOTODES

Beneficial nematodes are basically, tiny pest hunters that live underground. They control about 250 different types of insects, fleas being one of those. They do not harm the insects we need in our lawns and gardens, nor do they hurt earthworms. They are completely natural and one hundred percent organic. You can purchase them at Lowes, Home Depot, and even on Amazon.

The only drawback to using the name brand product is the cost. One million nematodes to cover 2000-3000 sq. ft. is nearly $40, while enough to cover an acre is nearly $70, and that is the cost if you do it yourself. To have the company itself come to your home and apply the nematodes is even more expensive.

I simply couldn't afford it. But like any other product, I looked for alternatives and found some. One of those was Dr. Pye's Scanmask Beneficial Nematodes ®. For about $18, including shipping, I could order 7 million nematodes, which was enough to cover about 12,000 sq. ft. Even buying two boxes, which was enough for my entire acre, was within my budget.

The same company that made using nematodes popular also makes a powder to be used inside the house. It is essentially borax powder and diatomaceous earth that has a low pH level and is said to be safer than using plain, borax powder. It must be applied to the entire carpet, including moving furniture. It is left for 24 to 72 hours and then vacuumed. It is said to be safe and natural. Since I have hardwood floors, I mixed borax powder and diatomaceous earth (1 to 1 ratio), and applied it in the corners of the two outbuildings set aside for the dogs and cats, and under any of the furniture or crates I had in either. I also applied it in out of the way places inside the house such as behind the washer and dryer, and in under the kitchen sink. I also applied it along the corners of the garage. It seemed very effective and I had no problems.

THE RESULTS OF MY FLEA BATTLE EXPERIMENT

By the end of the summer, I had reworked my plan. While the three steps (house, pet, yard) remained the same, what I used had evolved. As soon as the next spring arrived and before the fleas had a biting chance, I applied the beneficial nematodes to the yard. I continued to use DE in the garage, and outbuildings. Next, I had found that I could purchase a 3 month supply of Pet Armor ® Extra Large Dog 89-132 lbs. for around $15 including shipping on Ebay or Amazon. (Much better than $30). For me a 3 month supply treated all the dogs and cats once. Since I started with the nematodes and DE early, I only needed to use the Pet Armor about every 45 days instead of 30.

Below, you will see photos of the products I used.

Fipronil is found in products such as Frontline, or its generic equivalent PetArmor

Diatomaceous Earth (DE) must be food grade quality to use on pets Sells at TSC for $8.99 for 4 lbs or $12.99 for 20 lbs.

Thomas Labs Diatomaceous Earth kit called D-Flea. Comes with DE, flea comb and dust mask. A good buy at around $30

Borax powder with or without diatomaceous earth (1 to 1 ratio mixture) is an effective flea killer for carpets. Can also be used in and around baseboards. Test for colorfastness on carpets before application. Remove kids and pets while applying. Vacuum carpets in 24-72 hours.

Around $18 including shipping for enough nemotodes to cover 12,000 sq ft

CHAPTER 5

VACCINATION PROTOCOL RECONSIDERED

Vaccinating two dozen animals is not cheap. Thankfully, while still getting vaccines at cost while in California, I had vaccinated everyone before leaving. However, when the time did come for vaccines, I had some things to consider.

Contrary to popular belief, our pets do not need to be vaccinated for everything every year, and I knew that. At the time I was moving back to Tennessee, the veterinary vaccine protocol was starting to evolve. Extensive research had shown that immunity can last for years. One study conducted at the University of Wisconsin by Dr. Ronald Schultz and staff found that BOTH Rabies and Distemper immunity in dogs typically lasts about 7 years. For more information see:

(http://www.rabieschallengefund.org/education/duration-of-immunity-to-canine-vaccines)

A similar study on cats at Cornell University in the late 90's proved that cat immunity lasted about 7.5 years. (http://www.ncbi.nlm.nih.gov/pubmed/10328440)

Many veterinarians were hesitant to let their clients know about this research because they knew that it was only vaccinations that brought a healthy animal into a clinic. Most people will not take their pet to the vet for a yearly physical exam unless the animal needs vaccines. During a physical exam, many illnesses and/or potential problems are detected before they can do further harm. A dog or cat who misses a yearly physical is equivalent to a human going for ten years without seeing their doctor. So I understood the veterinarians' hesitation.

However, I also knew the mark-up on vaccinations and even though they are the staple of the veterinary clinic, I could not afford the mark-up price. So I determined what I needed, researched what was necessary in the area I lived in, considered possible vaccine reactions, and prepared an order.

The cost for each pet if going to a veterinarian would be approximately $50-75 if NO office visit was charged and vaccines only were received. If I did it at home, that amount would be reduced to about $10 per animal depending on how and where I purchased the vaccines and syringes.

Most of the animals I had at the time were over 5 years old with a few around 3 years. I decided my vaccine protocol would be to vaccinate yearly until 3 years of age, again at 6 years, and nothing but rabies thereafter. The reason for vaccinating with rabies after 6 years had nothing to do with efficacy, but the law of the state.

I have to be honest. At the time I could not afford to pay $10 each ($250 total) at a local rabies clinic to get two dozen dogs and cats vaccinated. I knew a company that would ship the vaccine to me even though it was not legal in my state to do it myself. I could vaccinate ten animals for less than $20. I knew that it would not keep us out of trouble if we were approached by animal control, but at least they would all be immune if approached by the wild life in our yard. It is most certainly, NOT something I would recommend and I won't mention the company name.

There are so many vaccines out there to consider. For dogs: distemper, parvo, Para influenza, infectious canine hepatitis/adenovirus, leptospirosis, coronavirus, lyme, bordetella, canine influenza, and even a rattlesnake vaccine. For cats: Feline distemper (pan leukopenia) , feline rhinotracheitis, calicivirus, chlamydia psittaci virus, feline immunodeficiency virus (FIV), feline leukemia (FeLV), feline infectious peritonitis (fip). And that doesn't even include rabies for everyone!!

Core vaccines are those given to most pets that cover the most common diseases. There are generally two kinds for dogs. Often called a 5 in 1, one vaccine covers parvo, distemper, hepatitis/adenovirus type 2, and Para influenza.. The second is the 6 in 1 which covers all the aforementioned, PLUS leptospirosis. My big decision in this case is did I want the lepto included?

I had always known the lepto in vaccines to be associated with reactions. Although more recent studies have shown it is no more likely to cause a reaction than any other vaccine, I hesitated. The studies HAVE shown that smaller dogs are more likely to have a reaction than larger dogs, and most of my dogs were ten pounds or less. So at the time, I decided no.

In addition to the 5 in 1, I did decide to administer a bordetella (kennel cough) vaccine yearly once we started taking in foster dogs. For some reason, the immunity of this vaccine only last for about 9 months, so it must be given more often.

So the dogs were taken care of. What about the cats? Although I did not move to Tennessee with the intentions of letting the cats be outside, eventually it happened quite by accident. I was always hesitant to have free roaming cats because of the diseases and danger they were exposed to.

Then one day the garage door opened at the wrong time and out went the cats. At first I started to panic, then I simply sat down and watched them. What a wonderful time they were having! No one was running away. No one ran to the road. They were the happiest I had ever seen them. I struggled with the decision and decided that in my family right now, happiness was very important, and if that meant the cats were outside, then so be it.

So what did that mean for their vaccines? Normally, if my cats had been indoors, I would have only vaccinated them with one core vaccine and rabies. However, since I worked in veterinary clinics for years, I had felt that I should vaccinate them for most everything. I changed that perception when evidence suggested that over vaccinating can do more harm than good.

However, at that time they had been vaccinated yearly with their core vaccine of a 4 in 1 which included pan leukopenia (feline distemper), chlamydia, rhinotracheitis, and calicivirus. I also vaccinated for feline leukemia (FeLV). I had hesitated to vaccinate for FIV in the past because a cat vaccinated for FIV will show up as positive for FIV on a FeLV/FIV test. If my cats were to ever get lost and be tested, it would be a death sentence most likely since FIV positive cats are generally euthanized.

After careful consideration, I decided on a protocol. Since all my cats were different ages, I vaccinated all with the 4 in 1 plus leukemia, until age 3, again at age 6, then nothing else but rabies thereafter.

THE UGLY SIDE OF VACCINES: IMPORTANT CONSIDERATIONS

One important consideration for me in regards to vaccines for my cats and dogs were what the vaccine itself did to the immune system. In a book I read years ago, Dr. Jean Dodds, a well-known expert on pet vaccines, was one of the first to clue me into the problem. I began to notice that many older pets came into the clinics where I worked with a few small issues, and the veterinarian vaccinated them. Within days or weeks, the pet would return with the small issues much bigger or with serious issues we had not seen before.

I came to believe that if an animal has an age related illness lurking in the background, the last thing you want to do is to challenge their immunity with a vaccine. According to the studies mentioned earlier, immunity lasts much longer than previously thought and in my belief (and many veterinarians), it is asking for trouble.

I also have misgivings about vaccinating puppies who have been exposed to the parvo virus. If the virus is already in the body, adding additional virus antigens and compromising the immune system seems counterproductive. Twice I have had shelter pups die from parvo within a day of being vaccinated. Some veterinarians agree with me, while others do not. It has always been an important topic in shelters and rescues as they face this same question every day. Even back in the 1990's when I was on the board of directors of a local humane society that ran a local animal shelter, it was a topic of hot debate. Let me explain.

Puppies have passive immunity passed down from their mothers that last only about 8 weeks. This is why most vaccines protocols have you begin vaccines at 6-8 weeks. As the mother's passive immunity dissipates, the vaccine begins to build up acquired immunity. If this is not started before heavy exposure to disease, what happens?

The standard parvo vaccine is a modified "live" virus, which means it is a virus that has been chemically or genetically weakened but is nevertheless viable or able to multiply in the host. A modified live vaccine (MLV) is known to be more effective than a “killed” vaccine which is a dead form of the virus plus an adjuvant to stimulate the immune system. The job of both is to elicit a response from the immune system so that when the immune system does “meet” the actual disease in the environment, it has “learned” how to fight it.

The problem occurs when an immunocompromised animal meets a MLV. The chances of getting the disease increases and the ability to fight it decreases. We already know that stress lowers the immune system. This is true in both people and pets. Imagine the stress of puppies in a crowded shelter environment. No matter how well maintained or how loving the staff, because of the horrid overpopulation problem, a shelter is going to be a stressful environment.

A pet shop will also be stressful with the crowds of people and busy shop keepers. An important note to keep in mind is that a large majority of puppies in pet shops come from “puppy mills” which are dog breeding facilities that operate more for profit than producing happy, healthy puppies. This is much like the smaller scale “backyard breeder”, in that the conditions are generally substandard (to say the least).

The needs of the pets in puppy mills and backyard breeders are often disregarded in order to maintain a low overhead. Even if vaccinated and dewormed, which is often in question, the environment and experience, and often poor breeding, creates an immunocompromised puppy.

It seems the safest and most prudent action should be to vaccinate most puppies with a killed parvo/distemper vaccine. Dr. Jean Dodds seems to agree. “I share the view of experts in the field that a properly constituted inactivated "killed" vaccine is always preferable to one of modified-live virus origin. The primary reason for this preference reflects safety to the host and the environment. Killed vaccines do not replicate in the vaccinated animal, they do not carry the risk of residual virulence, and do not shed attenuated viruses into the environment. Furthermore, killed vaccines do not bear the risk of contamination with adventitial viruses present in the tissue culture cells used to grow modified-live virus vaccines. Even if killed vaccines are proven to be somewhat less efficacious (produce lower levels or less sustained protection) than modified-live virus products, they are more safe. All killed vaccines on the market today have passed current efficacy and safety standards in order to be licensed for use by the USDA. In my view, therefore, medical professionals and the public should urge manufacturers to produce an assortment of killed vaccine products for use in companion animals. “
(http://devinefarm.net/rp/rpvaccin.htm)

As Dr. Dodds, mentions, we “should urge manufacturers to produce an assortment of killed vaccine products”. They are very difficult to find, particularly killed parvovirus vaccines. In the meantime, as a rescuer, I will determine individually, based on age, and former environment, whether or not I will vaccinate a puppy immediately. My other option is to isolate him/her for 14 days (the incubation period), to monitor for any signs.

While parvo vaccines are a concern in dogs, for cats the major concern is post vaccination fibro sarcomas. These are the cancers caused by vaccines that veterinarians have been noticing since the early 1980's. They occur in only about 1% of cats, but that number should still give you pause. I will never forget the day when I asked my boss, a veterinarian, why we were giving the vaccine in the right hind leg of a cat instead of the shoulder, and his answer was "Because it's much easier to amputate a leg than it is a shoulder." That, along with what I have learned about the extended immunity of most vaccines have been the inspiration for my change of vaccine protocol in my animals.

If you will notice, in many veterinarian offices now, there are protocols where the vaccine is given. This is so the veterinarians will know which vaccine caused a reaction or cancer. It is a sobering thought. So, I created my own vaccine protocol, keeping the vaccines to a bare minimum.

Vaccine Protocol for Dogs

DHPP (5 in 1) @ 8/11/14/17 weeks as a puppy, then every year until 3 years old, again @ 6 years & no more after that.

Rabies @ 16 weeks old, then as required by the state (every year or every 3 years)

Bordetella @ 17 weeks old then yearly if coming into contact with other pets (grooming/boarding)

***I intentionally stagger my vaccines in order to make it easier on the pet and not overload them at one time.*

Vaccine Protocol for Cats

FVRCP (4 in 1) @ 8/11/14/17 weeks as kittens, then every year until 3 years old, again @ 6 years & no more after that.

FELV @ 14/17 weeks as a kitten, then every year until 3 years old, again at 6 years and no more after that.

Rabies @ 16 weeks old, then as required by the state (every year or every 3 years)

*** All my cats have been tested for FELV/FIV as soon as I get them before they come into contact with my other cats. It is very important, and not a test you can do at home.*

CHAPTER 6

HEART WORMS AND INTESTINAL PARASITES

One of the most important lessons in saving money on animal care, is not to let your pet get sick in the first place. If there are things you can prevent, do it. One of those things is keeping your pet properly dewormed.

I knew both intestinal parasites and heart worms could do major damage to my pets. Intestinal parasites such as roundworms, hookworms, tapeworms, and protozoa such as giardia or coccidia could cause diarrhea, loss of appetite, lethargy, wasting away, anemia, and more. Heart worms could easily kill my animals and I knew that the treatment for heart worm was no longer readily available. Prevention could possibly mean life or death.

In the part of California where I had lived, heart worm was not a huge concern as I lived in a dry desert climate that did not encourage the propagation of mosquitoes. These are the carriers of heart worm, which can be deadly. Tennessee was a different story. Mosquitoes were everywhere. Luckily, I had been smart enough to have everyone tested before leaving California and I had purchased as much heart worm preventative as I could afford, which also protected against roundworm and hookworm. However, with the number of dogs I had to protect, that ran out quickly.

So I looked at the ingredients, and learned to dose it separately, but at a much lower cost. This was something that scared me initially. Treating heart worms with this new method was a bit scary. You always ask yourself, that if it was this easy, why doesn't everyone do it? I think the answer to that is the lack of education on the subject, convenience in giving one tablet, and a smart marketer who knows how to package and sell a product at a great markup. I found that to my surprise other vet technicians and even veterinarians had been following this practice for years. They were just too afraid or embarrassed to admit it. So what was the secret?

Ivomectin injectable marketed for cattle that could be given orally. It is the same ivomectin found in popular heart worm preventatives. In most of these preventatives, the dose is made to taste good and includes an intestinal dewormer, so the convenience and ease of administration is there. But those things cost me money I did not have. My choice was to leave my pets vulnerable to heart worms, or to give this method a go. So I did it.

IVOMEC FOR HEART WORMS
For $40 I purchased a 50 ml bottle of Ivomec ® 1% Injection for Cattle and Swine and a 1 cc syringe and an 18 gauge needle (because of the thickness of the liquid). Once a month I would mix the appropriate amount in the dog's food dish using this chart:

IVOMEC DOSAGE

Up to 10 lbs.	0.1 cc
11-20 lbs.	0.2 cc
21-30 lbs.	0.3 cc
31-40 lbs.	0.4 cc
41-50 lbs.	0.5 cc

and on as appropriate

I had no dog weighing more than 60 lbs. I used less than 2 cc a month which was a cost of about $1.60 a month for ALL my dogs for heart worm protection. At the very least using a popular heart worm protection product, that amount would have been $50 or greater a month.

My saving was at least $48.40 per month.

There has always been a caution on using ANY heart worm prevention on collie type dogs. For some reason they have a tendency to react poorly and it has known to cause death. My collie/retriever mix, Casey, has always been on heart worm preventative and has had no reactions on conventional preventatives or this method.

At this point, the subject of cats and heart worms is at a cross roads. It was once believed that cats are not affected by heart worms, but we have found that not to be true. We are also finding that it is more common than previously thought. The difference is in the way the heart worm reacts in the cat rather than the dog. Since the cat is not a natural host, the heart worm is generally unable to complete its cycle and make its way to the heart. It tends to migrate to the lungs where it can cause big problems. There are heart worm preventatives available for cats, but they are expensive, and to be honest, I have never worked for a single vet who recommended it. So for now, I do not use it for my felines.

The Ivomec takes care of heart worms, but I had to remember intestinal parasites in my dogs and cats. . Most prescription heart worm preventatives also come with an additional dewormer to cover those such as pyrantel pamoete or fenbendazole. Common names for these two dewormers are Nemex 2 or Strongid-t for pyrantel and Safe-Guard or Panacur for fenbendazole. I knew that fenbendazole took care of more types of worms (roundworms, hookworms, whipworms, and certain tapeworms) than pyrantel, plus it was a treatment for giardia, which is an intestinal protozoa that can cause terrible diarrhea.

PYRANTEL PAMOETE FOR INTESTINAL PARASITES

Years of reading fecal samples under the microscope taught me that the most common worms found in dogs and cats were roundworms and hookworms. That's why most veterinary hospitals use pyrantel pamoete as their drug of choice for deworming. Unlike when it is presented over the counter in pet stores where it is sold in a 4.5 mg/ml solution, vets purchase the 50 mg/ml liquid. The difference in cost is phenomenal. Since the larger milligram is sold for livestock in large doses (a quart bottle compared to a 2 oz. bottle for the 4.5 mg), the cost is only about 0.9 cents per ml compared to 0.30 cents per ml.

To treat a 10 lb. dog using the pet store purchased pyrantel, you would be using 5 mls of liquid, but only 0.5 mls using the livestock liquid (see chart below). The great thing I knew was this same bottle of pyrantel pamoete could be purchased at my local feed store if I knew what to look for. And considering it is almost impossible to overdose with Pyrantel, I knew it was safe. Some veterinarians I knew dosed at 1ml per 10 lbs. Their logic was higher was more likely to kill the parasites and since it would not hurt the animal, the small expense was worth it. So I followed that theory as well.

PYRANTEL DOSAGE
Using the 50 mg/kg bottle:

under 5 lbs.	.25-.5 ml
10lb	1 ml
20lb	2 ml
30lb	3 ml
40lb	4 ml
50	5 ml
60	6 ml

The first time I treated, I repeated the dosage two weeks later.

Deworming my dogs and cats using Pyrantel saved me a lot of money. Considering that I normally would pay at least $15 per animal at the vet hospital (not including office call and fecal test), the cost of the quart of Pyrantel at around $85 was a bargain.

Then I started thinking about whipworms, which are not controlled by Pyrantel. I lived in a rural area where not only did cats roam, but so did wildlife and, as I have said, prevention is much cheaper than treatment.

FENBENDAZOLE: MORE COVERAGE BUT HIGHER COST:
Fenbendazole is a big word for Panacur or Safe-guard. It treats all the same things as Pyrantel plus whipworms, some forms of tapeworms, and Giardia. Another advantage is not having to buy an entire quart, but plenty to do the job. I could by a 125 ml bottle for around $20 at Tractor Supply. It was marketed under Safe-Guard Goat Dewormer. I was paying about 0.16 cents per ml, which was an excellent price.

The disadvantage to the Fenbendazole, was that it had to be given once daily for 3 days. It also had a higher dosage requirement at 1 ml per 5 lbs. of body weight. So I had to give the following dosage for three days in their food.

FENBENDAZOLE DOSAGE

5 lb.	1 ml
10 lb.	2 ml
15 lb.	3 ml
20 lb.	4 ml
25 lb.	5 ml
30 lb.	6 ml
35 lb.	7 ml
40 lb.	8 ml
45 lb.	9 ml
50 lb.	10 ml

Mixed with a food and chicken broth, they didn't even notice. After the initial deworming, I changed to deworming with fenbendazole every three months while continuing to deworm with Ivomec once monthly.

PRAZIQUANTEL AND TAPEWORMS
As I said, fenbendazole will kill some forms of tapeworms, but NOT the most common one transmitted by fleas. Those are the ones that look like tiny pieces of dried rice near the tail. The only dewormer that would kill these worms is called praziquantel. Most people who get it at their vet office know it as Droncit.

These were the worms whose treatment was going to be out of my reach. Even buying over the counter tablets were expensive costing about $20 for 3 capsules. I would be lucky to treat 2 cats for that. I knew there had to be a better way. And I was right.

Fish Tape Capsules. The same exact praziquantel sold cheaper because it was marketed for fish. No prescription was necessary. At the time, I would need 26 tablets for my dog pack. For $30 I could purchase 30 tablets. Amazing the difference marketing makes.

That's $6.66 per tablet if marketed for dogs/cats OR $1.00 per tablet if marketed for fish.

Dogs require about 45 mg per lb. of body weight. Using 34 mg per capsule I dosed as follows:

PRAZIQUANTEL DOSAGE FOR DOGS:
5 lbs. & under – ½ tablet
6-10 lbs. –1 tablet
11-15 lbs. – 1 ½ tablets
16-30 lbs. – 2 tablets
31-45 lbs. – 3 tablets
46-60 lbs. – 4 tablets
over 60 lbs. – 5 tablets

The average cat only requires about 23 mg of praziquantel. The problem was I could only get the 23 mg capsule if I bought the one marketed for cats which was much more expensive. Since the fish tape worm capsules came apart, and one whole capsule was 34 mg, half of the capsule was 17 mg, and ¾ of a capsule would give about 25 mg. So I dosed the cats by putting it in their canned food and used the chart below using a 34 mg capsule:

PRAZIQUANTEL DOSAGE FOR CATS:

up to 10 lbs.	½ capsule
10 lbs.	¾ of capsule
over 10 lbs.	1 capsule

Deworming once is enough using praziquantel unless there is a re-infestation from another flea bite.

On the following page, you will see the products I used. All can be purchased at Tractor Supply Company with the exception of the "Fish Tapes" (Praziquantel) brand which I purchase from Countryside Pet Supply on Ebay or on their direct website.

Remember, when shopping for these products at Tractor Supply, do not look in the pet supply section, but rather the livestock aisle. It is much cheaper and comes in larger quantities, and often at higher dosages so less is needed.

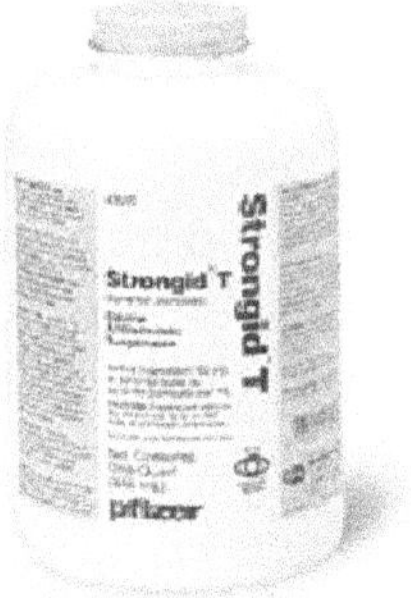

Pyrantel pamoate-also known as strongid-t and Nemex-2. Kills roundworms and hookworms.

Fenbendazole-also known as Safeguard or Panacur. Kills roundworms, hookworms, whipworms, and giardia

Praziquantel-also known as Droncit or Fish Tapes. Kills tapeworms caused by fleas.

Ivomectin-also known as Ivomec. Kills heart worms and is the main ingredient in all most heartworm preventatives.

CHAPTER 7

LAB TESTS I COULD DO AT HOME

FECAL TESTS:
One way I could tell if things were working as they should was to do a fecal test. I recall a day when it only cost $5 to get one at my local vet, but times had changed. Now a fecal test costs around $15 each and you often have to pay an office call. I had been reading fecal floats for years as a technician, so set out to figure out how to do it at home.

Amazing, what you can find on Ebay. I found several used microscopes for $25-100 and saved up my money. The next problem was figuring out how to make the fecal solution that would allow the worm eggs to rise, but the stool to fall allowing for a clean read.

Most vets use a product called Fecal-Sol ® for fecal flotations. However, by using water and Epson salt, you can make a similar product, so this is what I did.

I took a large mason jar used for canning and filled it about halfway up with warm water. I poured just a bit of Epson salt in at a time, and stirred until each one dissolved. When the salt would no longer dissolve, the mixture was ready and could be kept for a long time. If you would like to purchase a fecal floatation solution instead of making it, it can be found at Lambert Vet Supply under "medical supplies" as can many other useful products.

I purchased one hundred microscope slides and cover slips for about $5 from Drs. Foster and Smith Catalog. I had kept old pill vials from medications to use as my fecal vials. Using tongue depressors purchased or old Popsicle sticks I had saved, I took a small sample of the feces. I filled my vial to about half full, put the feces in the liquid and stirred. I then filled the vial to the top where it was nearly over flowing. Then I placed the slide cover on top and left it for 10 minutes.

Once the 10 minutes are up, I took the slide cover off and placed it in the center of the slide and placed it on the microscope stage. Starting at a power of 10x, I scanned for eggs. Most people I know go to the 40x lens from the beginning, but I learned to search this way, so it was easier for me. It was rare that I found anything.

One of the advantages of knowing how to do blood draws for lab work was that I could do my heart worm tests at home as well. The oldest method of testing is called a direct blood smear. All I needed was a tiny blood sample (just a drop) and I could put it on a slide, place the cover slip on top and look for micro filaria, or baby heart worms. An easy method of getting a drop of blood is to quick a nail, but I did it with a blood draw and a needle as I had been taught.

Normally this test is read with a microscopic strength of 40x. Although, not as good as some other tests, it had sufficed back in the 80's and 90's and in some vet offices, was still the test of choice. As of this writing, no tests have been positive.

This was how I knew my methods worked.

On the following page is an illustration of how I performed fecal tests. I have also included a photo of microfilaria (tiny heart worms). Learning to search for intestinal parasites and heart worms takes time and practice. One has to get used to differentiating between worm eggs and bubbles from the fecal solution. You also have to get used to the scale of the eggs or protozoa. Coccidia, for instance, is much smaller than a roundworm egg. Even after all these years of looking at fecal samples, I am still learning. Sometimes you will find things that will surprise you. Some examples of what I have found include different types of pollens and grain mites. It is always fun to discover something new. Additional charts and photographs of microscopic images can be found online. The more you practice, the better you become. I simply enjoy looking at various things microscopically. For instance, you will find a black hair looks blue under the microscope. There are so many new things to learn.

The cost of doing these tests using this method was a few cents compared to $15-20 each pet.

For the heart worm tests, I took a blood sample from the leg vein using a 1 cc syringe, however, I am experienced in doing so. Since only a small amount of blood is required for a direct smear, one option is to "quick" a nail. However, I don't recommend anyone not experienced with venipuncture to do this at home.

On the following page you will see instructions for doing fecal floats and direct smear heart worm tests. If nothing else, it helps to know what your vet is looking for when he/she performs these tests. The more you understand about your pet's health, the better.

At the end of the book you will find links to view in color, all intestinal parasites, heart worms, and more.

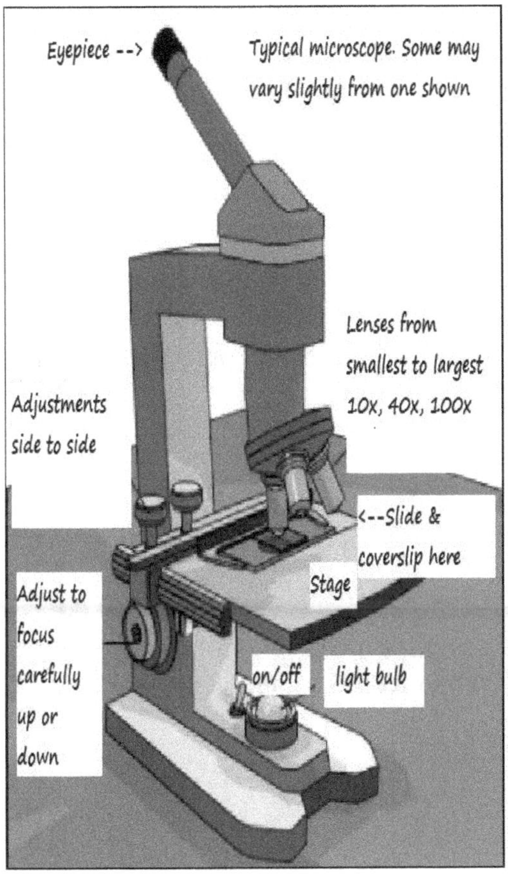

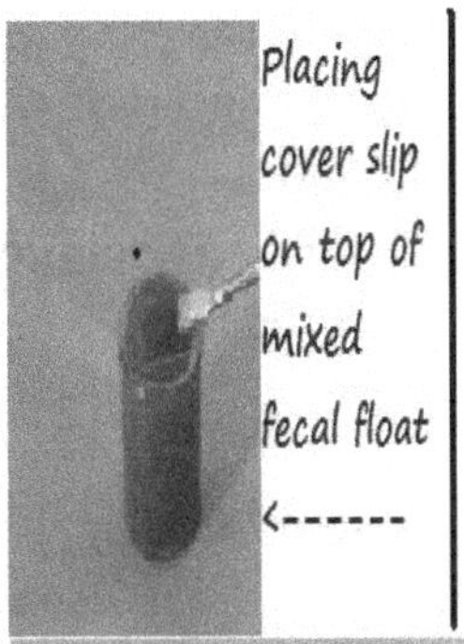

Fecal Floats:

Note: worm egg images not to scale. Not all eggs will be the same size as each other. Hookworms can be mistaken for tapes. Notice many small eggs within tape egg sack.

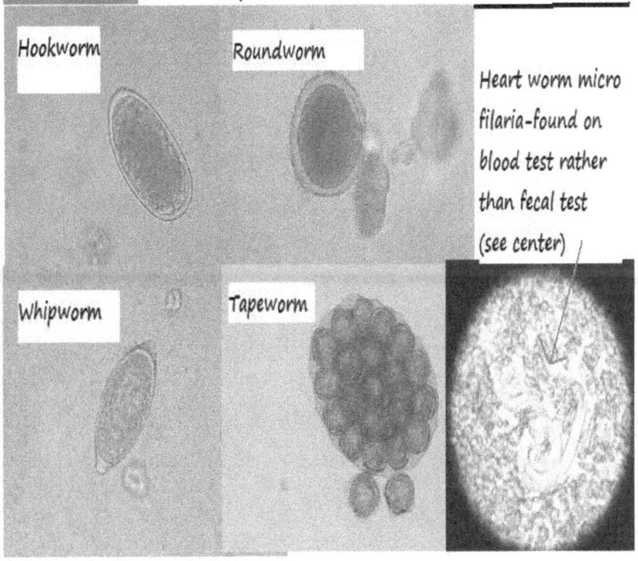

OTHER LAB TESTS AT HOME:
There were many other tests I could do using my microscope. For instance, I could take a skin scrape using the edge of a blade and look for demodex/sarcotic mange. With a quick purchase of Diff Quik stains on Ebay, I could also do an ear cytology looking for yeast and bacteria. Since I didn't have many problems with ear infections in my pets or mange, I didn't go to that extent, but it was good to know I could.

One of the things I did while a pet sitter and vet tech in California, was to go to homes on behalf of a veterinarian and take blood samples. Usually, this was for pets who were very fractious when at the vet and who were calmer at home. The most frequent testing I did was for blood glucose levels on diabetic animals. I still had my own glucometer which I kept in good working order in case my own pets started showing symptoms consistent with diabetes such as increased thirst and quick weight loss even with a good appetite. With the glucometer on hand, I would be able to know if their levels were at the proper 80-150 level.

I also kept urine test strips available as well. These are small paper strips onto which the urine of a pet (or human) can be tested for the following: Glucose, Bilirubin, Ketones, Specific Gravity, Blood, pH, Protein, Urobilinogen, Nitrite, Leukocytes, and Ascorbic Acid. It wasn't necessarily important to understand all the particulars of each value for my purposes. What it did was help me rule out a urinary tract concern.

There are many things that can affect the test and it should be noted that the urine I would collect would be contaminated. The only way to have uncontaminated urine is to do a cystocentesis where a long needle is put directly into the bladder in order to collect urine. Only an experienced vet should perform that procedure.

What I did look for mostly was blood and leukocytes, which are a type of white blood cell. Increased white blood cells indicate infection, while blood in the urine is always a concern. More on both in a later chapter.

CHAPTER 8

THE HOME PHYSICAL EXAM

One of the best things you can do for your pet it to know every inch of him or her. While not the easiest thing to do with two dozen animals, I tried to learn how to do a proper physical exam on each of my pets and to do it regularly.

If you pay attention when you go to the veterinarian, the doctor examines your pet in almost the same exact way each time. It is a practice ingrained in them to make sure they never miss any part of your animal.

The things I can do as a layperson is a bit different from the doctor. However, if I do the exam often enough, I will know when something has changed. So that's what I focused on doing.

Doing an exam like this from the time the pet is a puppy or kitten (which I rarely had), makes it easier to know what is normal. For me, most of the animals I had came as adults, and quite often, not in the best of shape.

It helps to know certain things that are fairly universal for most pets, such as temperature, pulse rate, breathing rate, etc. So I kept the chart below handy.

Temperature (dog or cat) 100.5-102.5 degrees
Heart rate Dog – 80-160, Cat 110-200 beats per minute
Respiratory rate (breathing rate) Dog 15-30, Cat 20-40 breathes per minute

On the following page is a diagram showing how to do a simple at home physical. As I said, it is not the exact same physical your vet will do. For instance, the vet can feel the abdomen and be more comfortable knowing if there are any abnormalities for that species. You, on the other hand, if you familiarize yourself with your pet's abdomen, can know if there are any abnormalities for your pet. That is just as important.

The most vital thing is to examine your pet often. Pay attention when you are petting him/her. Observe what a normal comfortable stance looks like so you will know when he is uncomfortable. Notice the color of her gums when she is feeling well, so you know when it looks discolored when she is ill. The more you recognize what is normal, the quicker you will recognize what is abnormal. Trust your instincts to tell you when something just “isn't right”.

Always feel the lymph nodes as marked with an "X" in the diagram. When these are swollen, it indicates that there is a possible infection. Checking it often allows you to be familiar with what is normal for your pet. It was Ms Ruby's swollen lymph node just behind her jaw that told me a dental visit could not wait.

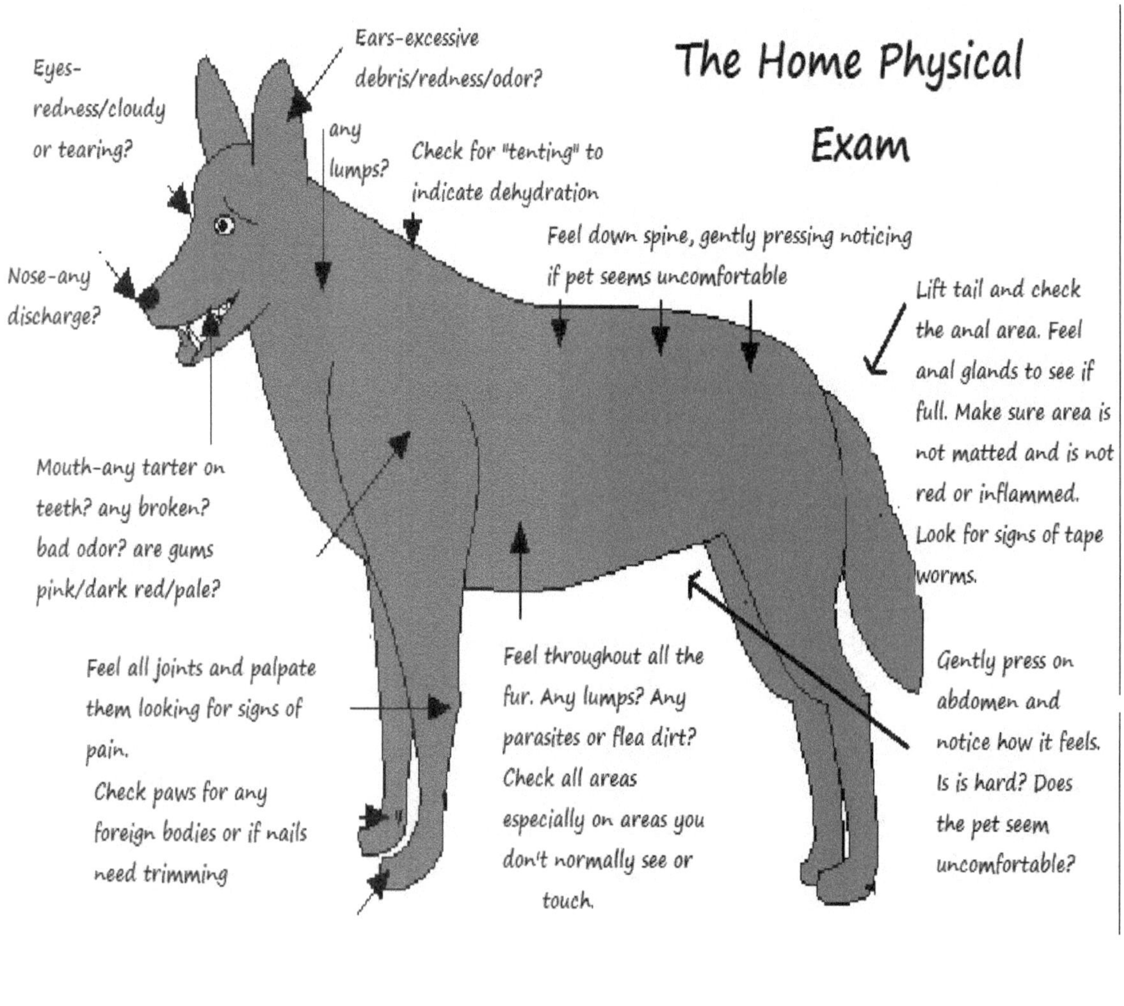

Another very important things I needed to check for was the mucous membrane color (MM), a fancy name for gum color, and capillary refill time known as CRT. The color of the gums should be a healthy pink as shown in the picture below. A reddish, inflamed gum simply indicates gum diseases such as gingivitis. Also keep in mind some dogs and cats have black pigment on their gums which is natural.

Mouth examination

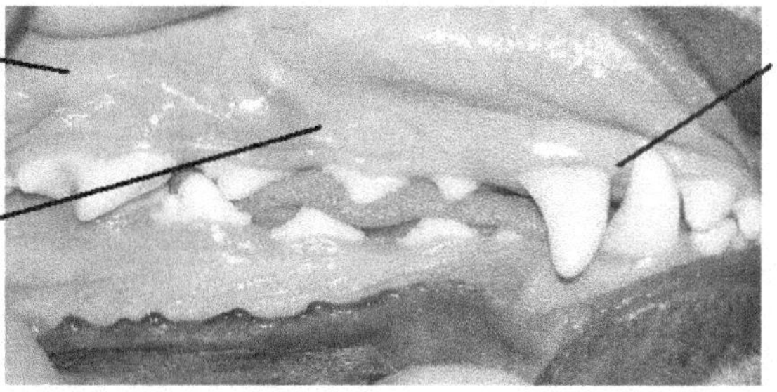

Yellow gums can indicate liver failure or disease. White or pale gums can indicate blood loss or the blood is not pumping properly through the system. Brick red gums can indicate bacterial infection, also known as sepsis. Be careful not to confuse this with gingivitis. Blue gums indicate hypoxia which means your pet is not getting enough oxygen. Any unusual color needs attention quickly.

Sadly, most often times I have seen white or pale gums is in puppies with parvo. The parvovirus, which causes bloody diarrhea, was particularly widespread when I worked in a clinic serving the poor in San Bernardino, CA. I can't tell you how many times I had to look into the eyes of a parvo puppy, and into its mouth, to see the white gums, and confirm by test, that the puppy had parvo. More often than not, there were not enough funds to treat the pet and I was the one who had to put him/her to sleep. It’s an experience I would like to forget.

On to capillary refill time. CRT is done by pressing onto the gum and letting go, counting how many seconds it takes for the now-white gum to return to its original color. It should take less than 2 seconds. Any more than that and your pet is probably dehydrated.

To confirm dehydration, pull up the skin on the back of your pet's neck around the shoulder blades (typically called the “scruff”). This is checking the skin turgor, or elasticity of the skin. The “tent” of skin you have pulled up should return to normal immediately upon letting go. If it doesn't, your pet is dehydrated. (More on dehydration later).

GROOMING TIME AS PART OF THE PHYSICAL EXAM

A great time to do a physical exam is when you are grooming your pet. It is very important. It allows you to look for parasites and growths and to remove matted fur. People often underestimate the damage matted fur can cause. During my time as an animal cruelty investigator, I came across so many animals who had been left to mat and who were unable to defecate as the hair was so tight, it held the feces inside. Others were unable to move properly without pulling at the hair and skin causing rips and tears. In the summer, we would shave the mats from these dogs to find maggots eating through the skin.

So brushing the fur regularly on your pet, not only keeps him/her looking good, but is good for the pet and saves you money in the long run. You will spot little problems before they are big ones, and if you do have to take your dog to the groomer, it will be much cheaper to trim an unmatted pet compared to a matted one.

One of the ways I have saved money is by learning to groom at home. Although it is not a show dog look, a little practice makes acceptable. Scissoring is not something I have ever been able to learn, but I can do a summer shave down. Although there is controversy over whether shave downs are a good idea, my dogs love them. I also have one cat who gets in line voluntarily. It also allows you to get a very close look at areas of the body you can't normally see. For instance, when I shaved my dog Scrappy this past spring, a growth was revealed that I wouldn't have seen otherwise. I had it removed immediately before it became cancerous.

The key to doing a good shave down or "summer cut" is getting good quality clippers. I personally love Andes ® clippers and they come in many affordable styles. My preference is to have a clipper with blades I can change rather than using combs. It's much faster and easier. The only blades I use are the 10 blade and the 7 blade to blend the fur.

There are many good instructional videos on YouTube and grooming books with instructions. However, for me, it was a process of on the job training. Using a 10 blade, I always start about an inch behind the ears and trim most everything but the head, tail and legs. Then I switch to a 7 blade and blend those areas I had not touched. It's as simple as that. I did have to learn what areas to be careful in. Anywhere where the skin tends to be thin, I take my time and go carefully.

Part of the grooming routine should also include a nail trim, anal gland expression, and ear cleaning. Instructions for doing all three follow in the next several pages.

NAILTRIMS

Dogs and cats should be taught from the time they are little to allow you to touch their paws. In my case, I rarely had my pets early on. Some of the chihuahuas in particular were terrified of nail trims, so it took a lot of patience and work. Each individual pet is different. Some did better if another person held them for me, while others felt safer in my arms while I served as the trimmer too. Don't be afraid to do a nail or two, give them a treat, and sit them down to play. Eventually, they see it as a good thing. Making a big presentation of it is rarely in your favor. The only exception to that has been Mr. Buster who loves to hear the words "Buster it's nail trimming time!" To him that means "belly rubs". Whatever you can do to make something awesome happen at nail trimming time, life will be easier.

Occasionally you will come across a black nail that doesn't allow you to see the quick. If the pet has any clear nails, observe where the quick is in the clear nail and normally the quick will be about the same place on the black nail. If no clear nails are available, clip in small increments. When the nail begins to feel more spongy and thicker, you are probably close to the quick.

For nails that are extremely long but also have a long quick, you will need to clip the nails more often for a while. When you clip close to the quick, it will recede. Each time you clip again, it will recede more. Do NOT intentionally quick the nails when the pet is awake. If you've ever "quicked" a nail, you know how much it hurts. It is cruel to do that to anyone. If you have it done while under anesthesia, ask for pain medication for later. Just because an animal doesn't show pain, does not mean he/she doesn't hurt. Remember, it is their natural instinct to hide pain.

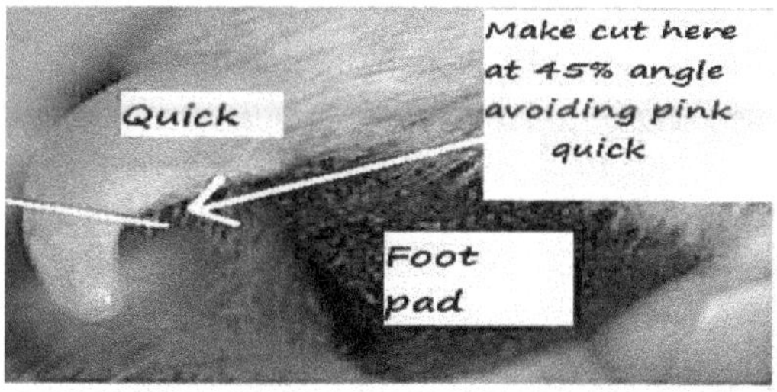

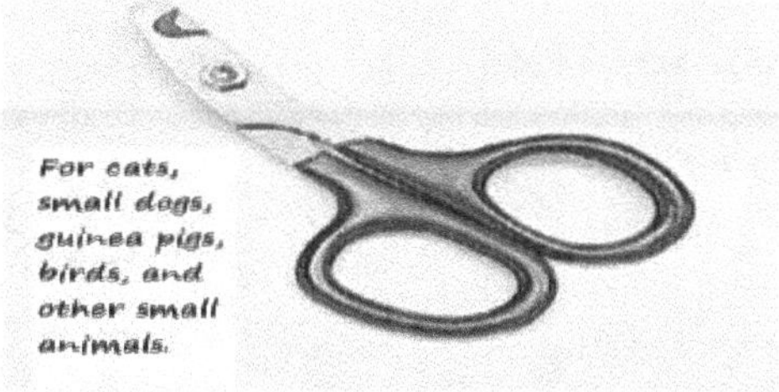

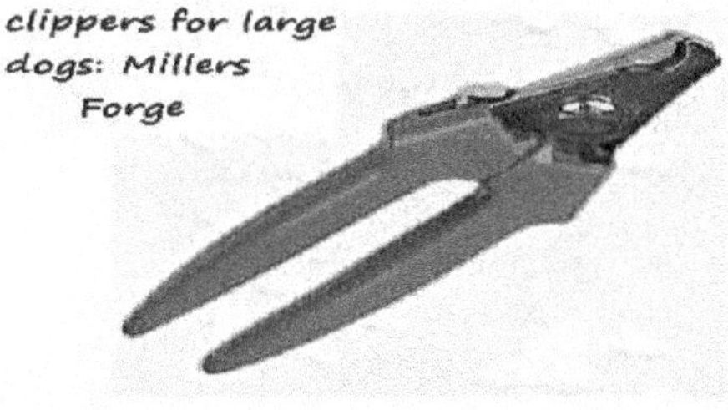

ANAL GLANDS

If you have ever seen your dog scooting his booty on the carpet, chances are his anal glands are full. No one really knows why the anal glands exist, but to our chagrin, they do. The anal glands are located on the anus at about the 4 and 8 o'clock position. They fill up with a vile fluid, that, if it fills in excess or with fluid that is too thick, will abscess. In other words, somewhere around the gland pocket, it will rupture, leaving a hole. It is a painful, painful thing.

It is best to express the anal glands each time you bathe your dog. I've never seen a cat with this issue, so it is not necessary to worry with it.

Fair warning from a vet tech: Be sure, when expressing the glands, to put a paper towel over the area and point it away from your face.

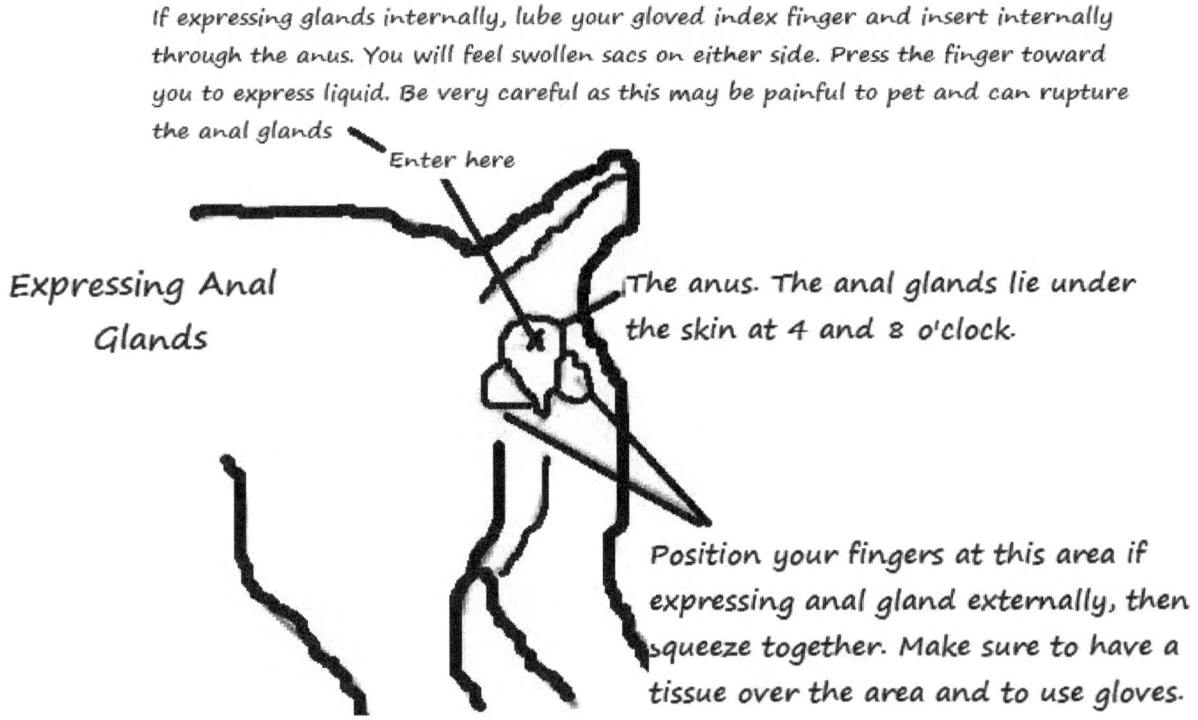

EARS

Cleaning the ears of a dog or cat is a fairly easy procedure. The trick to keeping the ears clean and healthy is to keep a fairly acidic environment in the ear canal. This discourages yeast and bacteria from growing. One of the easiest methods of doing this is to mix apple cider vinegar and water in a 1:2 mixture. You want to have enough to flood the ear canal, so I add ½ cup of vinegar to 1 cup of warm water and put it in a squeeze bottle or use a large syringe.

Holding up the ear flap, I use a 6 cc or larger syringe, or the squeeze bottle to gently force the fluid into the ear. The pet will want to shake his/her head, so I flush quickly, put the ear flap down, and immediately massage at the base of the ear. Let the pet shake. If there is no debris, you've done enough. If there is, you can use a cotton ball to wipe the area clean, and repeat the flush until no more debris is present.

Keep in mind that the ear of the dog and cat is much different from ours. The ear canal is in the shape of an "L". Unlike humans, where it is a fairly direct route from outer ear, to ear drum, in canines and felines, it is not. Wax and debris can become impacted, making frequent cleaning necessary for some. Normally cats have little issue with wax and debris unless they have ear mites, which are more common in cats than in dogs. The debris is typically black and often resemble black sand. It is important to clean the ears before applying any medication for ear mites.

Back to cleaning. Since there are so many crevices in the outer ear, I do use q-tips to clean the outside. It is much harder to damage the ear drum in either species because of the "L" shape, but you can push the debris further down, if you are not careful.

In some dogs, hair grows densely in the canal. This can cause lots of problems. It can attract and hold in debris and wax, and it also helps to keep the inner ear moist, which is the perfect environment for yeast infections. If your pet does have this issue, it is very important to pluck the hair regularly. Most people use a powder made of boric acid (not the same as Borax) to sprinkle onto the hair first. This makes it easier to grip. If the hair is long enough, you can pluck using your fingers, but if not a hemostat is required. The hemostat locks down onto the hair. Then you twist it several times and pluck quickly. If you have your dog professionally groomed, ask them to do it for you and if your pet is going to be under sedation for any reason, that is also a good time to have it done. Just a note...I have never met a cat with this problem, so no plucking.

Dogs with ears that hang down, like basset hounds, for instance are particularly prone to ear infections. Air flow is limited allowing moisture to build up. Add that issue to a dog like a retriever that loves to play in water, and you can have the makings of a lifelong ear infection. Cleaning them regularly with a vinegar solution will make the canal more acidic. An acidic environment is the enemy of yeast and bacteria.

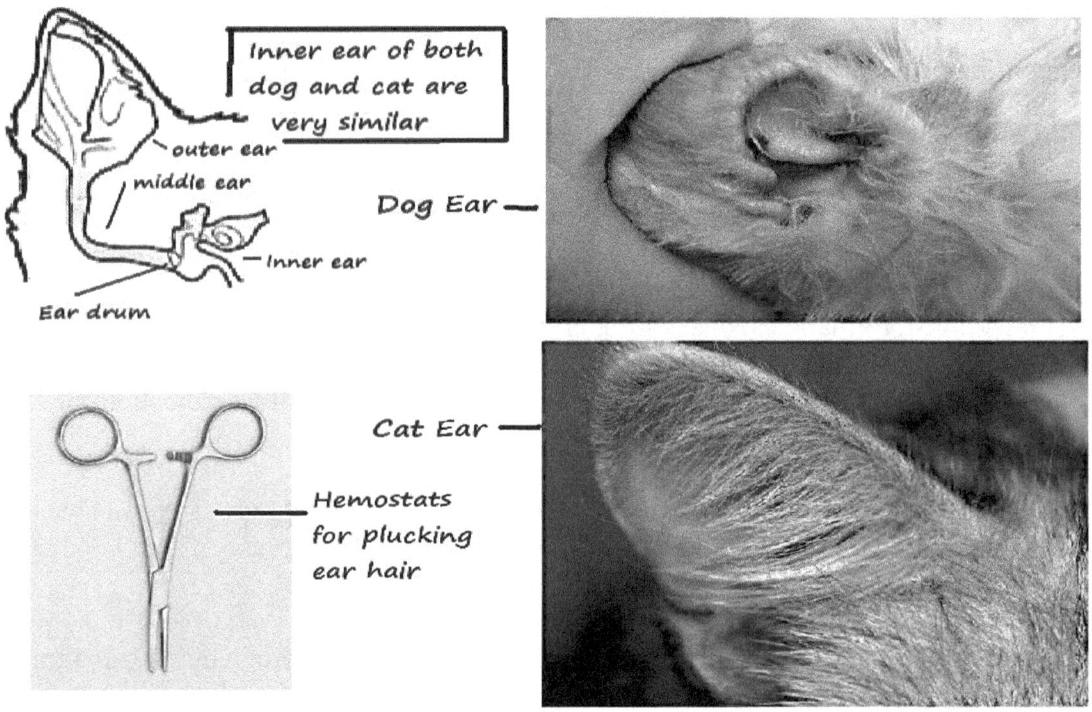
Inner ear of both dog and cat are very similar
outer ear
middle ear
Inner ear
Ear drum
Dog Ear
Cat Ear
Hemostats for plucking ear hair

CHAPTER 9

WHEN AN EXAM REVEALS A CONCERN: COMMON ILLNESSES

Physical exams can reveal a lot of things. Determining what is an emergency or something just to take note of, takes practice. You may find a swollen area on the skin for instance. If it is a lump that you can get your fingers around, showing it is not attached to muscle, it is most likely a fatty tissue cyst. If it is firm and attached to the underlying tissue, it may need a biopsy. If it is red, inflamed, and warmer than the surrounding area, it is probably infected and may be an abscess. Learning what is normal is essential to learning what is abnormal.

FEVER:

If I question whether or not my animal feels well, one of the things I do is check for a fever by taking a temperature rectally. In a quiet dog or cat (one who has not been exercising), a temperature exceeding 103 degrees should be addressed. There are many reasons for a fever. It is not uncommon for pets to have a low grade fever for 24 hours or so after vaccinations. Infection is another reason, and it is a good idea to search the body head to tail looking for any open wounds or abscesses.

One way to bring a fever down is to wash the paws with alcohol. I keep a few twelve oz. soda bottles filled with water in the freezer for times like this as well. I have wet the fur down on my pets before in hopes of reducing the fever. Putting a fan on them is also a good idea as is wrapping him/her in a cool, wet towel. Depending on the situation, I may give them one appropriate dose of Nutri-Vet Canine Aspirin. However if there is any form of intestinal upset involved, I do not give aspirin and I never give an aspirin to a cat. As soon as a vet is available, it is important to have the pet checked.

VOMITING AND DIARRHEA

There are so many different causes for both that it can be difficult to pin down. In the times I have noticed my pets vomiting, the first thing I do is take away their food. If they are vomiting and gulping water, I take away the water. As mean as that seems, it is a tried and true veterinary tactic. We call it NPO which is the Latin equivalent of "nothing by mouth" (nil per os). There is nothing better than NPO to stop the cycle. If you do offer water, do so in very small amounts.

If I have ruled out intestinal parasites and protozoa, I consider what they have eaten in the last 24 hours. If they are only having diarrhea with no blood present, I will give them one loperamide (Imodium). It is not weight dependent, but should only be given once in 24 hours.

If they are vomiting a yellow bile, and do not seem in distress, I will give them famotidine

(Pepcid) according to the dosage chart I keep in my pet medicine cabinet.

If after 24 hours, the pet feels like eating, I boil chicken and mix with white rice. This is similar to the formula found in Hills Prescription I/D ® which vets recommend to gently return the pet to eating. It should be given in very small amounts several times a day rather than large amounts a few times a day. Over the next few days, slowly mix in the pet's regular food.

INTESTINAL BLOCKAGE AND BLOAT:
If a dog is eating, but vomiting and NOT having diarrhea, pay very close attention. Feel the abdomen, and see if it feels painful. Check the mucous membrane color. Notice if the pet is pacing or seem uncomfortable.

There are two things that cause me quite a bit of worry in cases like this and I have seen both occur. One is a blockage. The dog eats a sock or a toy and it gets stuck, allowing nothing, or very little through. Or, a dog eats or drinks a large amount, and the stomach twists (commonly called gastric torsion or bloat). Both of these are absolute emergencies and you do not wait around to see if it gets better on its own. Either of these can cause a very painful death. They cut off the blood supply to the stomach and intestines. I have seen far too many pets die this way. Keep in mind that cats can swallow things as well. I have seen cats in distress from swallowing needles and string. Never wait if you suspect this. One life saving procedure I have witnessed is a pet parent suspected bloat and gave his dog two Gas-X tablets before rushing to the vet. Although there was no absolute proof it saved the dog's life, the vet told the pet parent it was a very wise thing to do. I wish I had thought of it when my little guy nearly killed himself.

My personal experience with this came one day when I came home to find my male basset hound mix, Buster, looking very very pregnant. His tummy was huge. I went to the food cabinet and found he had consumed all the dog food. All of it. I rushed him to the vet I worked for. Somehow, his stomach had not twisted. How, I do not know. He was put on medication to help the food process through the intestinal tract a little easier, and spent quite a bit of time in the dog potty for the next few days.

DEHYDRATION
Another cause for concern is dehydration and the reason for it. When “tenting” the skin near the neck reveals that it takes several seconds for the skin to return to its natural position, it is an emergency.

Dehydration has to be addressed fast before it gets any worse. If you've ever been dehydrated (and I have), it is a horrible feeling. Your body doesn't respond as it should. You feel dizzy, nauseated, and lightheaded. Severe dehydration leads to death. In times when I could still get my dehydrated pets to drink, I would mix their water with something like Pedialyte ®. But to be honest, I find the taste pretty disgusting, so I have found a solution that seems to work well. The recipe is below. When I serve it to the pet, I normally heat it until it is barely warm. This seems to stimulate their senses.

TREATING DEHYDRATION ORALLY

With those warnings heeded, there are times when dehydration hits, and you have to do something about it. When the pet will not drink, there is really only one thing to do. I can't tell you how many times I have taken in a foster animal only for it to come down with parvo after being removed from the shelter. For some reason, it always seemed to happen on a Sunday when the vet offices are closed. For that reason, I decided to always be prepared. The first 12-24 hours are the most important. Below is a recipe for treating dehydration orally. Re-Sorb can be purchased at Tractor Supply, while the bouillon can be purchased at your local grocery.

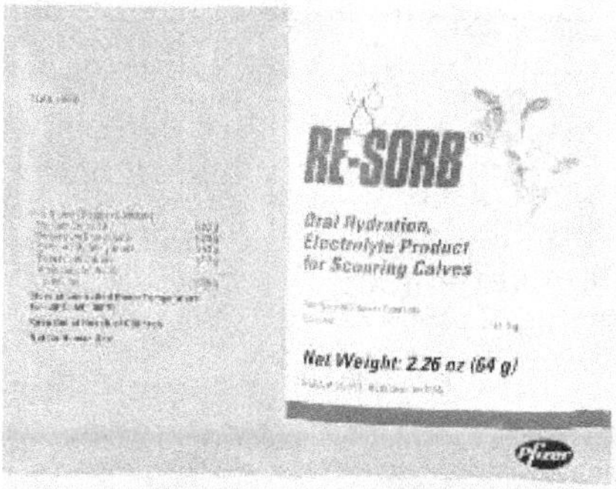

Add 1 bouillon cube to one (1) cup of hot water. Mix until dissolved. Put contents in pitcher. Add enough warm water to make 2 quarts. Add the entire contents (both sides of of Re-Sorb packet) and stir. Once it cools, it can be used as a dehydration remedy to give my mouth. Store excess in refrigerator.

ADMINISTERING SUBCUTANEOUS FLUIDS

If the pet were at the vet, he/she would have an IV catheter installed with fluids going directly to the vein. That is the best possible way to treat dehydration. The next best thing is subcutaneous fluids, often called sub-q fluids. Later in the book, you will see more specifics about where I have purchased the supplies for doing fluids this way. On the following page, you will see the method I use.

I have dosed my pets at 5-10 ml per lb. of body weight. Depending on the weight of the pet, I am careful not to put too much fluid in one area. Since the skin of dogs and cats are different from people, there is quite a lot of room to stretch, but common sense is necessary. Normally about 100 ml's/cc's is enough in one area.

Ms. Pearl, a 2 lb., 2 year old chihuahua came to us after she and her three brothers and sister were taken out of the shelter. Normally a dog her age will have developed plenty of resistance to most puppy diseases, but Ms. Pearl had none. She came down with Parvo within the week. This is the method I used for her:

In the areas circled, I pulled the skin up in a "tent" fashion, inserting an 18 gauge needle in the "door" of the tent. Once it is inserted, I continued to hold the tent up a bit, which allowed the flow of the fluids. Once I turned on the fluids with the flow control, I watched the fluid reservoir just below the bag to see how quickly my fluids were running. If the fluid ran slowly and pulling up on the "tent" didn't improve it, I pulled back slightly on my needle and repositioned it. If that didn't work, I had to remove the needle and try another area.

I realize that using the large 18 gauge needle seems painful, but it works best at getting the fluid in quickly. The elasticity of the canine and feline skin deals with needles in a much different way than tight, human skin. For most pets, the quicker you can get the fluid in, the better they will deal with it. They also handle the fluids better if they are warm. Its a good idea to lay the bag on a heating pad for a while before administering them.

In the illustration on the following page, I have used a feline, but the locations and method are the same for both dog and cat.

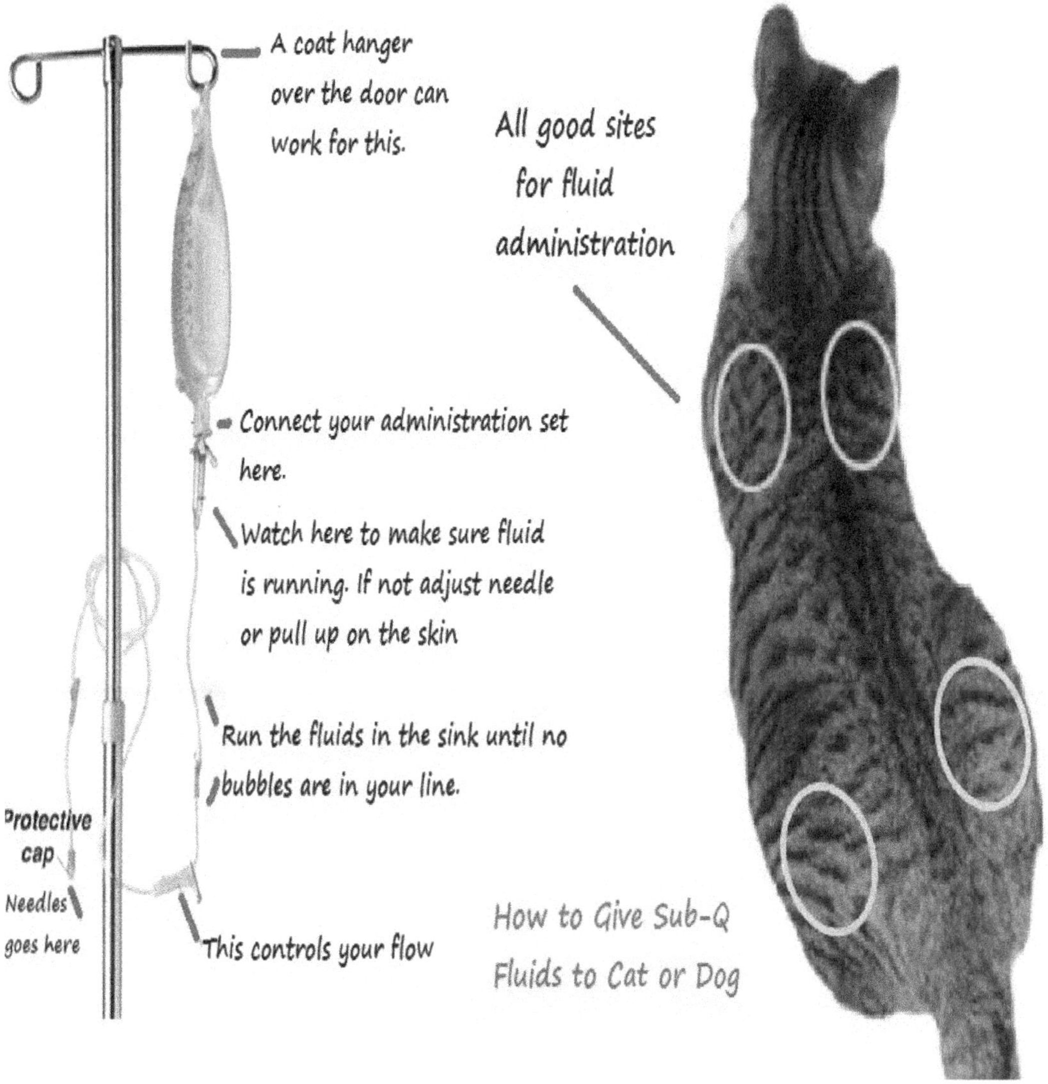
A coat hanger
over the door can
work for this.
All good sites
for fluid
administration
Connect your administration set
here.
Watch here to make sure fluid
is running. If not adjust needle
or pull up on the skin
Run the fluids in the sink until no
bubbles are in your line.
Protective
cap
Needles
goes here
This controls your flow
How to Give Sub-Q
Fluids to Cat or Dog

CAT ABSCESSES
Another emergency that came on a weekend was a cat abscess. These abscesses are normally caused by a bite or scratch from another animal. Cats can get abscesses most anywhere. On the face, side, neck. The longer the abscess stays intact, the worse the infection can get and the sicker the cat will feel.

My cat Peaches, who normally never fights, developed an abscess one Sunday. I prepared everything I would need including my clippers, a surgical steel #10 blade used for surgery, a bowl (to catch the infection), gauze to clean the area with, a 12 cc syringe, and a Nolvasan ® solution made by mixing 1 part Nolvasan to 2 parts warm water. I shaved the area using my clippers and a 10 blade (not to be confused with the surgical steel blade used to make the incision). Normally, veterinarians shave with a 40 blade on their clippers to get the shave surgically close, but a 10 blade was the best I had.

Sometimes, when you shave an abscess, the wound will open up and drain on its own, but it did not for her. So I took the surgical steel #10 blade, and near the bottom of the abscess, pressed the blade in. (This is the EXACT procedure I have assisted with as a vet tech). Depending on the amount of infection (how swollen it looks), you may need a disposable bowl to catch it in. It is not something for the easily sickened. Once the infection had drained, I cleaned the area with Nolvasan ®. Using my Nolvasan/Water solution, I filled up my 12 cc syringe and flushed the wound several times. I then filled it with a bit of Triple Antibiotic Ointment.

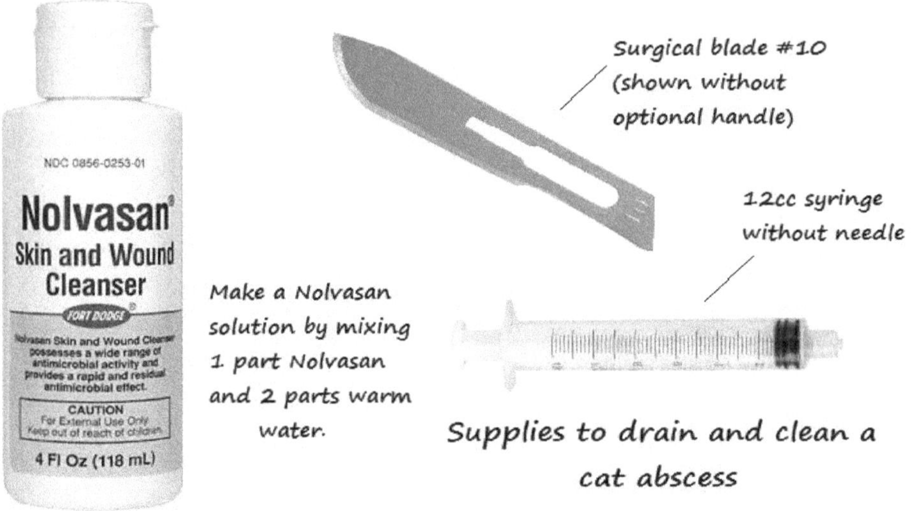

Supplies to drain and clean a cat abscess

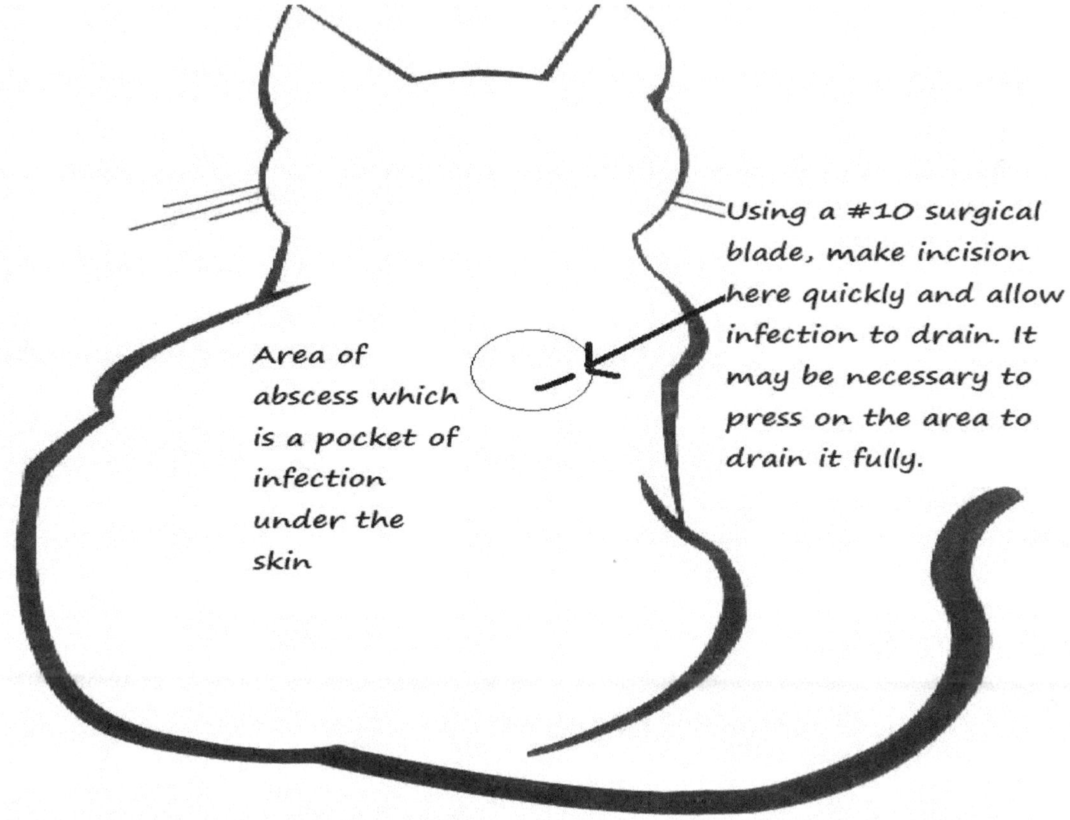
Using a #10 surgical blade, make incision here quickly and allow infection to drain. It may be necessary to press on the area to drain it fully.
Area of abscess which is a pocket of infection under the skin

OPEN WOUNDS AND STRAINS
No two wounds are alike, but there are certain universal things that can be done. I have dealt with bite wounds, scrapes, cat scratches and more. In my days as an animal cruelty investigator, I even had to deal with severe burns on a dog whose owner poured boiling water on him.

The first thing most veterinarians do with wounds (and the first thing I do as well) is to shave the area surrounding the wound if possible. If the skin is burnt, be very careful not to touch the area of the burn. I always make sure my clipper blades are cleaned and sterilized before and after.

Next, I clean the area with my 1:2 Ratio Nolvasan ® solution, mixing Nolvasan and warm water. Then I apply a Triple Antibiotic Ointment or Nitrofurazone to the wound. (More on these medications and solutions in a later chapter). Not all wounds need to be bandaged, but if they do, use a non-stick gauze pad.

For strains and sprains, I keep a product called Vet Wrap ® at all times. This can also be used as part of your bandage for open wounds. It is similar to an ace bandage, but it sticks to itself and is much more stable.

Recently when my Pomeranian Panda, jumped a few too many times, he injured his front leg. I bandaged it by using tape stirrup strips on the front and back of the leg (taping parallel to the leg). The tape strips are made twice as long as the leg and a popsicle stick or something similar can be put between the excess tape to keep it from sticking. I wrapped the leg once with gauze and then again with Vet Wrap. I then twisted my stirrup tape and stretched it up the leg to keep the bandage from slipping.

One of the best descriptions on how to bandage wounds is found online at:

(http://www.eu.elsevierhealth.com/media/us/samplechapters/9780750688079/9780750688079.pdf)

This link provides detailed instructions and photographs to teach you proper wound management and dressing. I printed it out and keep it in my pet medical supply cabinet.

On the following page you will find a diagram of the simple bandage I made for Panda. I made sure to monitor the bandage to make sure it didn't cause any rubbing. I have seen bandages do more harm than good especially when a splint is used. The rubbing can cause open sores and be very painful. After a week, I removed the bandage, but he still had a bit of a limp. I re wrapped and one week later, he was back to normal.

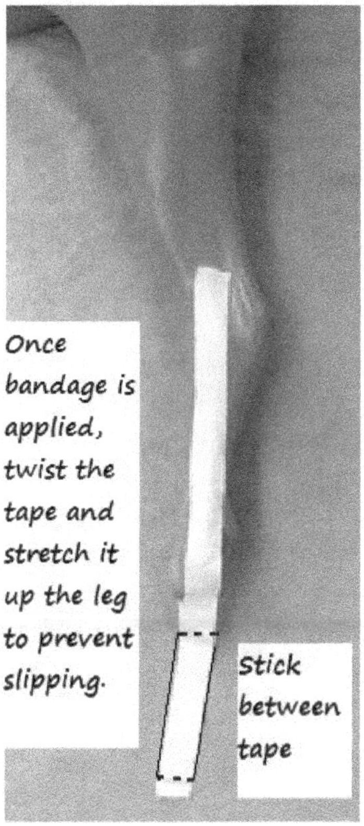

To do a very simple wrap for a sprained leg, apply stirrup strips to the front and back leg as shown. Put something like a popcycle stick between the tape to keep them from sticking to one another. It is best to apply a layer of gauze around the leg first beginning from bottom to top before applying your Vet Wrap using the same pattern. Once the Wrap is complete, twist the tape around so that it sticks to the vet wrap itself. This will keep it from slipping.

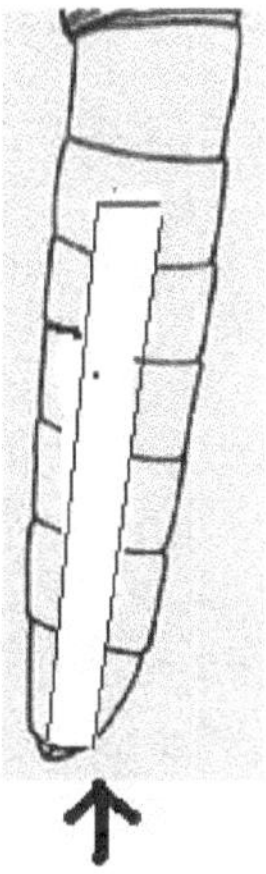

The end result will look similar to this.

UPPER RESPIRATORY INFECTIONS (URI):
One of the most common illnesses in the feline is an upper respiratory infection. It can be viral or bacterial in origin. Similar to our head colds, a cat with URI may sneeze, have nasal congestion and/or discharge, have eye drainage and even conjunctivitis (swelling of the mucus membrane or pink part of the eyelid).

There are generally four causes of URI. It helps to know the different symptoms so the best treatment and isolation can be assured.

- Herpes- fever, depression, loss of appetite, drooling, eye ulcers, lethargy, sneezing, eye and nasal discharge. Discharges may be more prevalent with herpes.

- Calici- oral ulcers, lameness, signs similar to herpes, only milder

- Chlamydia- mild sneezing, serious eye infection, called conjunctivitis

- Bordetella- fever, sneezing, lymph node enlargement, nasal discharge, harsh lung sounds and cough.

If the nasal and eye discharge is clear, sometimes simple home treatments can help matters until the immune system does its job. If a cat is experiencing nasal congestion, for instance, you can put him/her in a small room with a vaporizer. When my oldest cat, Chloe started having a dry cough, I brought her in and put her in a small room with a vaporizer. I didn't have a heating pad at the time, so I put my bearded dragon's heat lamp on her at night. It made a tremendous difference and in less than a week, she was completely better with no medication given.

One product that helps cats who have a stuffy nose is called Little Noses ®. It is a saline nose spray, normally used on newborn humans. Only one or two drops in each nostril once daily should be given. Good nursing care, such as wiping discharge away from the nose and eyes, is also beneficial.

An important thing to remember with cats: If they cannot smell, they will not eat. It is vital that a cat eat to avoid hepatic lipidosis (fatty liver syndrome). One trick I have used when cats are dealing with congestion is to lightly heat canned food. This increases the aroma making it easier for the cat to detect. If the cat is avoiding drinking water, I also will often add a little tuna juice or chicken/beef broth to the water.

Viral infections must run their course and are not treated with antibiotics. However, with the immune system busy, secondary opportunistic bacterial infections will take advantage. Normally a vet will prescribe a tetracycline or doxycycline antibiotic and request the pet be quarantined.

URINARY TRACT INFECTIONS (UTI):
Urinary tract infections are not uncommon in either dog or cat. Symptoms include blood in the urine, unusual frequent urination and/or frequent attempts at urination without urine production, and urinating in inappropriate places.

While both dog and cats can get kidney and bladder stones, they affect the pets differently. I have seen golf ball sized stones removed from the bladder of small female dogs before, yet the dog was still able to urinate. However, in a male cat, a small crystalline stone the size of a grain of sand can block his urethra, making him unable to urinate, resulting in death within 24 hours. Size of the urethra in relation to the stone make a big difference in this case.

I mention this first before discussing a general UTI to reiterate that as soon as you suspect a male cat having any urinary tract issue, do NOT attempt to treat at home. Generally, a urinary catheter will need to be passed if the pet is blocked in order to save his life.

Also keep in mind that in older dogs, incontinence can occur without an infection. Just like people, as the body ages, the bladder becomes harder to control. The drug of choice for incontinence is Phenylpropanolamine (PPA). It is not an expensive drug and works very well.

With that said, as soon as I see any of my animals (except the male cats) showing any possible symptom of UTI, I collect a bit of the urine with a small flat bowl and test the urine using urine testing strips discussed in the chapter "Lab Tests You Can Do at Home".

If the results of the tests show leukocytes (white blood cells) or blood, be concerned. There is no way to rule out kidney or bladder stones without a x-ray. More specific urinalysis testing can be done by your vet who will often prescribe antibiotics such as amoxicillin or ciprofloxin while awaiting the results.

A good way to help prevent some urinary problems is to add potassium citrate with cranberry to their food. Some will simply add Cranberry extract that you can purchase at any health store.

It's also important to make sure your pets drink plenty of water. Some pets like running water, particularly cats. While you can buy pet water fountains, they are very expensive. I figured out an inexpensive way to make a water "bubbler" that my cats enjoy.

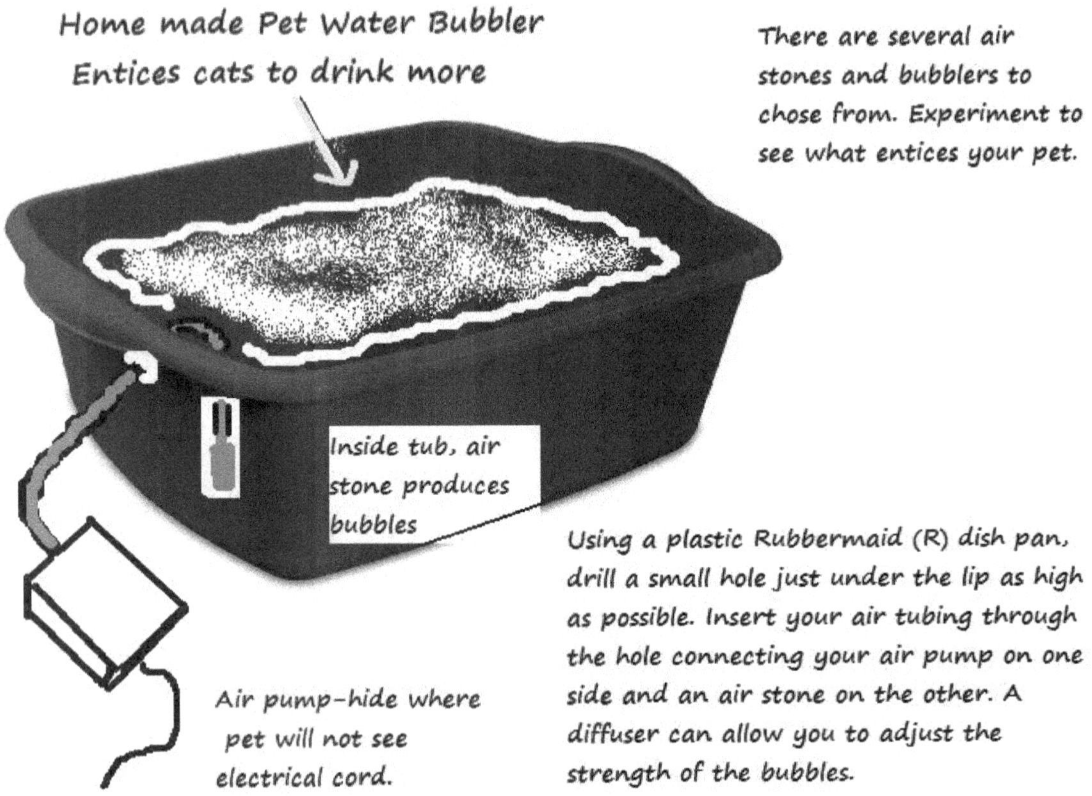
Home made Pet Water Bubbler
Entices cats to drink more
There are several air stones and bubblers to chose from. Experiment to see what entices your pet.
Inside tub, air stone produces bubbles
Using a plastic Rubbermaid (R) dish pan, drill a small hole just under the lip as high as possible. Insert your air tubing through the hole connecting your air pump on one side and an air stone on the other. A diffuser can allow you to adjust the strength of the bubbles.
Air pump-hide where pet will not see electrical cord.

EAR MITES AND INFECTIONS:
Although both dogs and cats can get ear infections, it is much more common in dogs. For cats, the typical issue is ear mites.

Ear mites are tiny microscopic bugs that feed by piercing the skin. As described earlier, ear mite debris looks much like black sand. They cause intense itching and head shaking. They can easily be passed from one cat to another, including mother to kitten.

To diagnose ear mites, a swab of the debris is taken using a cotton tipped applicator. Apply one drop of mineral oil to a microscope slide. Place the tip of the swab in the mineral oil and spread as evenly as possible across the slide. Starting at 10 x power, read your slide, moving up to 40 x power. If mites are present, they can be seen moving around in the oil. Under the microscope, and ear mite will look like this:

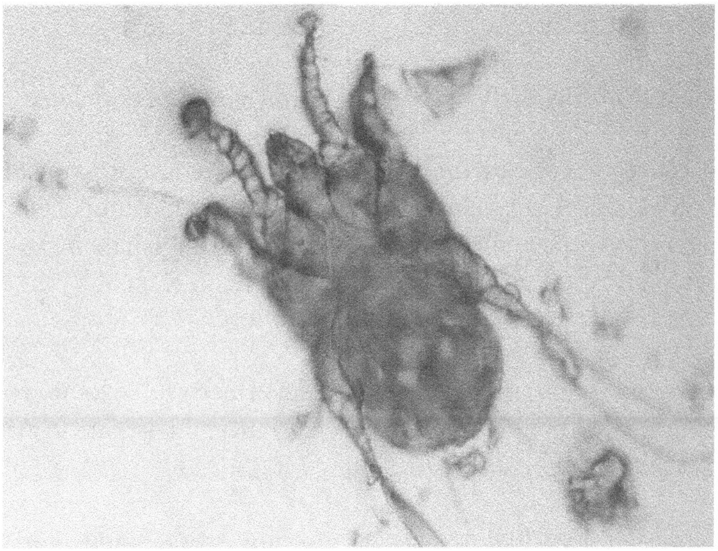

After cleaning the ears, I apply a homemade the ear mite treatment.

HOMEMADE EAR MITE TREATMENT: (similar to Acaraxx 0.01% ivomectin)

You will need a measuring cup and a 3 ml syringe. Pull up 1.2 ml of Ivomec 1% injection for cattle and swine. Add the ivomec to the measuring cup first. Add warm water to the ½ cup mark. This will be 118.8 ml of warm water. Put contents in plastic squeeze bottle. Shake very well. Draw up 1cc of the mixture per ear. Apply to each ear holding ear closed once applied. The cat will attempt to shake, but it is best to hold closed at least thirty seconds. The application should not need to be repeated unless the cat is an outdoor cat that becomes reinfested. You can dispose of the remaining liquid or keep for future use.

Although dogs can also have ear mites, it is not very common. Generally, their issues are either bacterial or yeast related. Yeast is the most common and is caused by having a wet, moist environment in the ear. Dogs with floppy ears are more prone because their ears do not allow the proper air flow to dry out the ears. This is why regular cleaning with a vinegar/water solution creating an acidic environment is so vital. Yeast infections have a very strong and noticeable odor. However, the only way to be positive if it is a bacterial or yeast infection is to do an ear cytology. While possible to do at home with the right equipment, I have found a solution I prefer.

The most common veterinary treatment for ear infections is called Otomax ®. The ingredients in Otomax include an antibiotic (gentamicin sulfate), an anti-fungal/yeast (clotrimazole) and an anti-inflammatory (betamethasone). A similar product can be made at home using nitrofurazone, clotrimazole, and hydrocortisone cream. For more information about the ingredients, please see the chapter regarding a pet medicine chest.

HOMEMADE EAR INFECTION TREATMENT (for bacterial and yeast infections)

Take 1 part nitrofurazone, 1 part clotrimazole, and 1 part hydrocortisone cream. For instance, 1 tablespoon of each. Mix thoroughly. Put in an appropriate sized squeeze bottle. You may need to clip the tip off the bottle for the medication to come through. The nozzle on the bottle will allow you to put the medication far down into the ear canal. Repeat twice daily for 10-14 days. Clean ears at least once daily with vinegar water solution.

An optional treatment (although perhaps not quite as effective), is to alternate using clotrimazole cream and nitrofurazone powder (NFZ Puffer). Use one in AM, one in PM and clean ears again, thoroughly once daily.

In severe cases of ear infections that just are not getting better, some veterinarians will put dogs on an antibiotic, such as Cephalexin if an ear cytology reveals it is more bacterial related, and even sometimes when bacteria is secondary to a yeast infection. For stubborn yeast infections, the drug of choice is Ketaconazole.

There are times when ear infections are secondary to other issues. In other words, it's not the primary issue. For instance, food allergies can sometimes manifest themselves in recurrent ear infections. Hormonal issues can also make one more prone to infections.

Another possibility is the presence of a foreign body. In California, with every spring, there came a massive explosion of foxtail cases. Foxtails are common weeds whose seed dispersal comes as a unit. They have a hardened tip and barbs that point away from the tip. Once on the pet, they can burrow anywhere. I have removed foxtails from between the toes, from the inner ear, the nostrils, and even from behind the eye. They can cause abscesses as well. So if you see your pet pawing at his/her eye, nose, or ear and you live in foxtail country, rule out a foxtail first.

One thing to note about both ear mites, ear infections, and foreign bodies is the possibility of an aural hematoma. These are basically a swelling of the ear caused by the constant shaking of the head. Fluid begins to fill up within the traumatized area. The only treatment is to drain the hematoma, surgically stitch it in such a way that it cannot fill up again, treat whatever the cause of the irritation was to begin with, and follow up with antibiotics. It is not something that can be done at home because it requires anesthesia. It will need to be drained, then tacked with sutures in order to prevent it from filling up again. The repair and healing of an aural hematoma is a long process that requires multiple vet visit. Rarely will the ear look the same after healing. It is so much better to prevent than to treat.

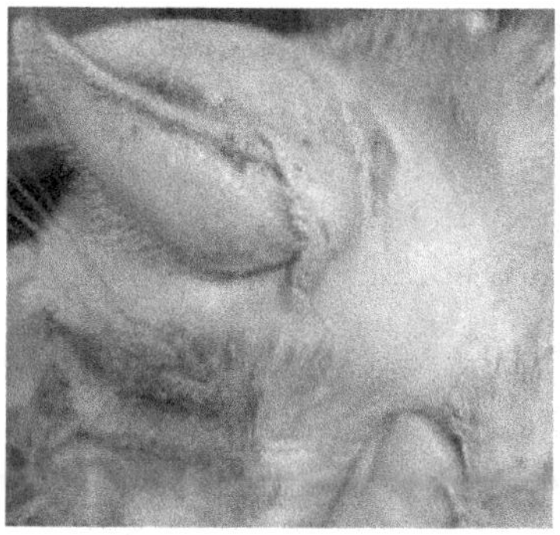

Aural Hematoma in a cat

Foxtails

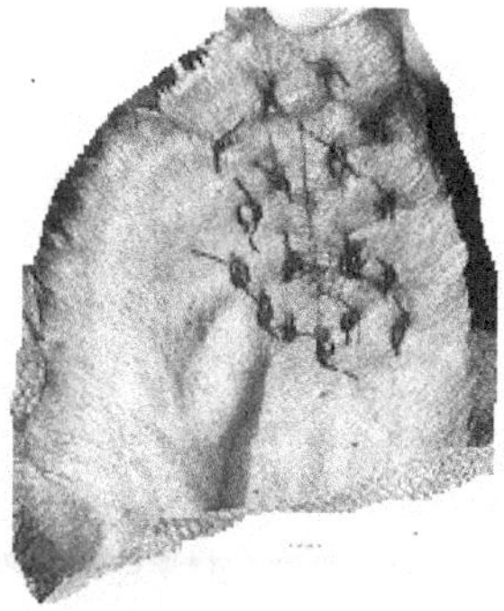

Hematoma surgery post drainage

SKIN ALLERGIES:

Other issues you might find upon examination is skin allergies, hot spots, and alopecia (hair loss). It's important to keep in mind that things that make humans sneeze, tend to make our dogs and cats itch. There are several causes of allergies in our pets.

CAUSES AND TREATMENT OF ALLERGIES IN PETS
OTC=over the counter, RX=prescription*

ENVIRONMENTAL/SEASONAL – Many are allergic to lawn grass and pollen. Problem seems to worsen during times of high pollen counts in the early spring and autumn. Owners tend to notice pets licking their paws, abdomen and other areas that touch the ground.

- Treatment: over the counter (OTC) medications such as diphenhydramine (Benadryl), chloraphenaramine (Chlor-trimeton), prescription (RX) medications such as hydroxyxine, cyclosporin (Atopica)

FLEAS/TICKS/MANGE MITES-Only fleas and ticks can be seen with the naked eye. A skin scrape analyzed under a microscope will reveal demodex or sarcoptic mange. Demodex mange is an overgrowth of mites that are already normally on the body. It is an immune problem that often resolves itself. It does not spread from animal to animal, but siblings can both be affected. Hair loss is patchy and the skin normal looking. Only the sarcoptic mange is transmutable to humans and other animals. .Symptoms include extreme itchiness, loss of hair and red, scaly skin. For flea allergy dermatitis, the itching is most often focused near the base of the tail. Fleas do not have to be present at the time for the allergy to take place. The saliva from the flea can trigger a reaction that can last for a while. Ticks rarely cause itchiness, but can cause lyme disease, so they should be removed immediately.

- Treatment – The treatment for fleas and ticks are covered in a previous chapter. For demodex, the pet needs to be bathed in a Benzoyl – Peroxide Shampoo and then dipped in amitraz which is found in Mitaban ® dip and allowed to dry (do not towel off). This should be done at least once weekly until skin scrapes reveal no more mites. There are times when oral Ivomectin must be given when the dips are not successful. Sarcoptic mange is treated with weekly baths and a lime-sulfur dip. Selamectin, which is sold as Revolution ® is a topical similar to Frontline ® that helps kill the mites. It is recommended to use it at least for 2 months (once per month). For both demodex and sarcoptic mange, it is best to shave the pet to a summer cut while treating. The dip can reach the skin easier and it will be more comfortable for the pet.

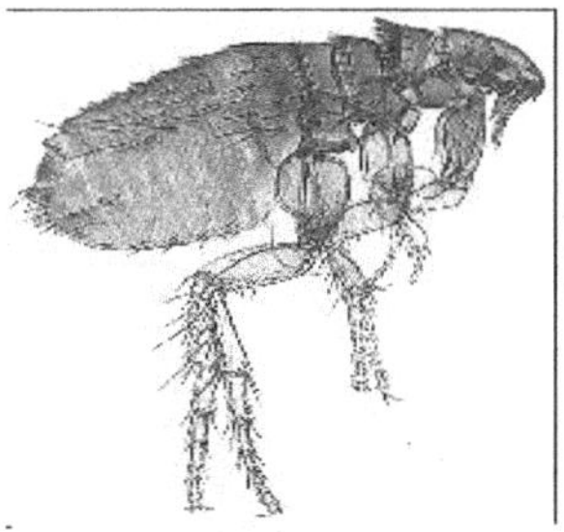

FLEA (not to scale)

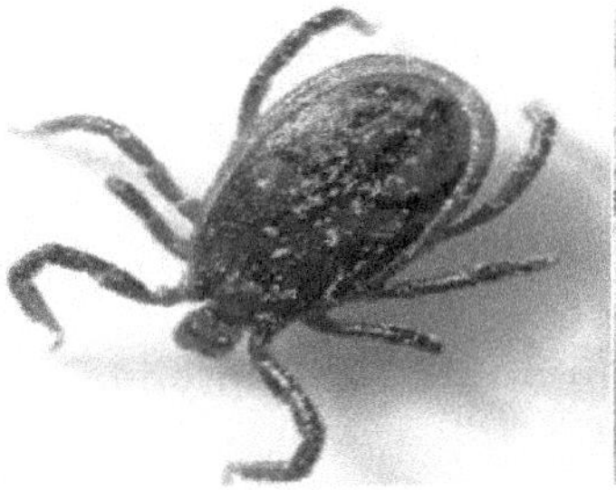

TICK (before feeding)

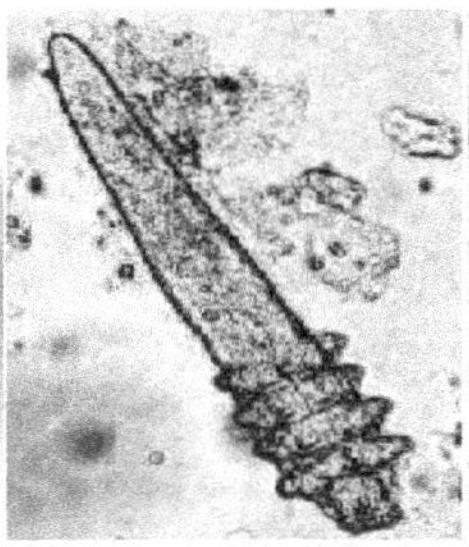

DEMODEX MANGE

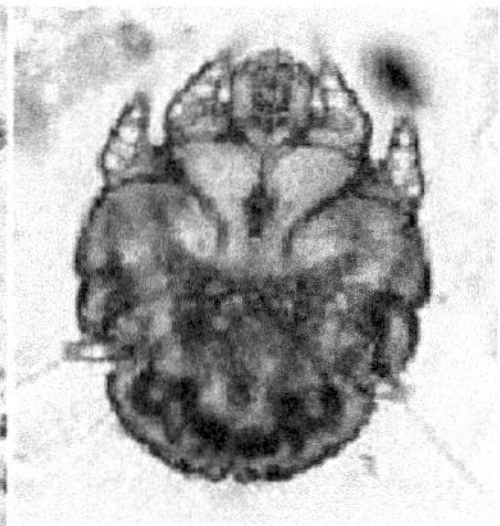

SARCOPTIC MANGE

FOOD ALLERGIES-Pets can be allergic to the grains, meats, and fillers in pet foods. The itching is rarely localized and does not change with the seasons. Gastrointestinal problems may also occur. Cats with food allergies will often scratch around their head and face. (Be sure to rule out ear mites in cats). Dog will scratch at their faces, chew on their feet, and may get frequent ear infections.

- Treatment: If you suspect a food based allergy, look to see what the main ingredients are in the food you are feeding. Typically you will find some type of beef or chicken. In the new food you choose, the two things you want to look for are the meat source, and the carbohydrate source. My first food of choice for food allergies is a fish and rice based diet. There are also fish and potato diets, venison and potato, chicken and rice, and even rabbit and rice, and duck and potato. Some of these diets are prescription only foods. Iams makes a fish and rice diet which can be purchased without a prescription. It can take a while to isolate what is in the food that the pet is allergic to. When food changes are made do it gradually in order to avoid stomach upset. Some vets recommend feeding the new food for 2 months, then going back on the old food to see if there is a reaction, but in my opinion, if it's working, leave it alone.

SKIN INFECTION-skin infections can be caused by bacteria (pyoderma), yeast (Candida) or fungus (ringworm).Bacterial infections usually present as pustules, hair loss, and redness. The classic lesion is circular with hair loss and crusty on the outer edges. Yeast infections tend to occur in moist areas such as the skin folds. The skin tends to be a little more greasy and red, the smell more pungent, and the skin tends to thicken. It is a very common culprit in ear infections. To positively identify between bacteria and yeast requires testing the skin. The most common fungus is ringworm. Ringworm is not a worm. The name came from the small circular lesion it leaves. It is more common in cats than dogs. It is difficult to diagnose without doing lab work which can take several weeks to get results. The lesions are small circular areas of hair loss. Vets often use an ultraviolet light source called a woods lamp ® to see if the lesions fluoresce.

- Treatment- Medicated shampoos: Malaseb ® (for all) Povidone Iodine (fungal/bacterial only) Keratolux ® (all), Oral Medications: Cephalexin or Amoxicillin (Bacterial), Ketoconazole (Yeast), Essential Fatty Acid Supplement (all) Ointments: Nitrofurazone (bacterial), Clotrimazole (Yeast/Fungus)

SEBORRHEA – Occurs when the sebaceous (oil) glands produce too much sebum. Can make the skin excessively oily, dry and very flaky, or both. There is often an overabundance of scaling or dandruff. Typically occurs most along the back, but because it creates a great environment for yeast and bacteria, problems can be anywhere on the body. It is often secondary to other problems, particularly hormonal problems such as Cushing's disease.

- Treatment – It is important to rule out hormonal issues with a thyroid test. Often, bacterial and yeast infections accompany seborrhea, so often the same shampoos, ointments and medications can help. One of the best shampoos on the market is DermabenSs ® made by Dermapet.

HOT SPOTS – A hotspot is basically an area of skin that has become so irritated, red, inflamed, and itchy, your pet can't leave it alone. Some dogs will lose hair, while others will not. If you see that your pet is obsessing over a particular area, gently pull the hair back. The area may be a bit bloody and raw.

- Treatment – Clip the fur surrounding the hotspot. It will keep the fur from tickling the area, make applying medicine easier, and also allow the wound to dry out. Clean the area with a Nolvasan ® and warm water mixture (1:2 ratio). Apply Nitrofurazone to the wound. I prefer the powder. If the hot spot is in an area a doggie t-shirt will cover, I put one on the pet. Some vets suggest wrapping the area with a bandage and spraying the bandage with a deterrent like Bitter Apple ®, but I use that only as a last resort. Other items I use with a hotspot is Wonderdust ® (see medicine cabinet chapter for more information) If the wound is not yet raw or open, but extremely itchy, I apply a hydrocortisone cream or Gold Bond ® Medicated Cream or powder. If you bathe the dog, use an oatmeal based shampoo and cool (not cold) water. If this does not cure the problem, sometimes a steroid injection or oral medication like Prednisone may be needed. Never use an otc hot spot medication containing alcohol as they will sting and cause more irritation. If the dog refuses to leave the area alone, you may have to purchase an e-collar or Bite Not ® collar so that they cannot reach the area.

E-collars are the lamp shade plastic collars that you can purchase from a veterinarian or from local pet stores. For smaller pets like little chihuahuas, they can be made with a little card board. I personally hate them because the pet knocks over everything in his/her path. With some animals, they are the only good solution. Whenever possible, however, I use a Bite Not Collar. This collar can be purchased directly from their website or for many other distributors.

They are not as easy to find as e-collars and you may have to order one online. If so, a temporary solution is diagrammed on the following page. My recommendation if you have only one or two pets, is to go ahead and purchase the real thing when you are able. You will need it sometimes during your pet's lifetime.

TEMPORARY HOMEMADE BITE NOT ® COLLAR: Until you can purchase the real thing (which will most definitely work better) fold a thick towel (or dish cloth for tiny dogs) longwise, wrap it around the neck and tape it using a strong tape. You can also put a larger regular collar over the towel to hold it in place. The purpose is to keep the neck from turning completely around to reach the wound. Cardboard can also be used, but may cause some skin irritation. Get the real thing as soon as possible.

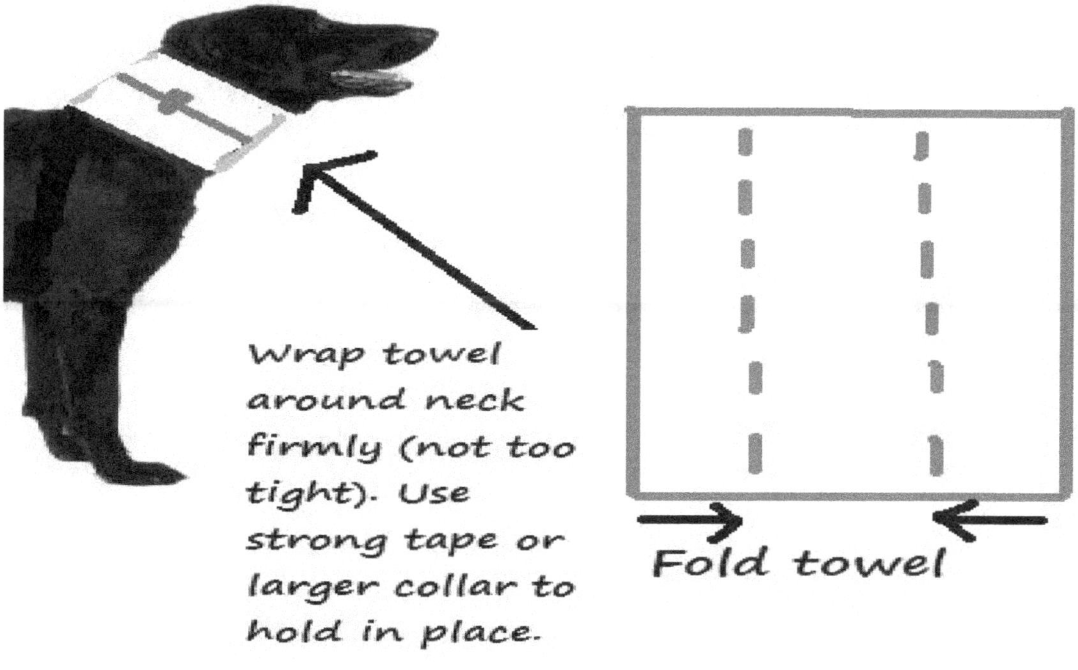

BEHAVIORAL/NEUROGENIC – Some pets lick, scratch, and bite out of nervous habit. Often these pets are bored, lack exercise, or suffer from separation anxiety. Lick granulomas are often caused by neurogenic issues . The dog will lick at his/her paw for instance until all the fur is missing.

•Treatment – Finding out the cause is the number one issue. Make sure the pet gets plenty of exercise and interaction. Most medications used do not treat the skin, but the anxiety. The most common is called Clomicalm ® or its generic equivalent, clomipramine. A vet may still need to prescribe medication for irritation caused by the constant chewing and scratching. If you are not home for long periods of time, consider leaving the television on, getting a second pet to keep your first one company. Buy him/her a toy that requires work and thought to enjoy, or a bone that takes a lot of licking to get to the center goodies. There are many such ideas in pet catalogs such as Drs. Foster and Smith.

Another issue of concern is if a pet has no feeling in an extremity or tail. Once, while working in down town New Orleans, a dachshund, who had nerve damage in his front right paw, chewed the paw nearly off. Not only did he need to be put on medication for the obsessive chewing, his paw had to be wrapped and eventually amputated. Animals do not seem to miss extremities as we do. They adapt so much better. If a leg or tail has lost all feeling, allow the vet to amputate. Wheelchairs for pets work great and can even be home made using pvc pipe. A good source of information and ideas is www.handicappedpets.com.

CHAPTER 10

MY PET MEDICINE CHEST

Taking care of this many animals meant staying organized and well prepared.

One of the things I learned as a veterinary technician was to keep a well-stocked pet medicine chest and first aid kit. It was easy when I had access to a vet clinic. Before leaving California, I had purchased quite a few medications that I knew I could use. Once I was no longer working for one, and had gone through my supply, I had to think outside of the box.

One of the keys in doing this was to realize that sometimes, the same medication can be marketed many different ways, and you often pay quite a lot more for the marketed product. For instance, almost all human sleep aids are simply diphenhydramine, otherwise known as Benadryl, usually sold as an antihistamine. The marketers prey on your need for sleep, put it in a box marked "sleep aid", and you buy it.

I also learned not to rely on "kits" put together by companies and sold as "pet first aid kits". Those are great to put in the car and keep while hiking with your dog for instance, but for my purposes, I would have been paying a whole lot for great packaging.

So, using my head, researching like crazy, and thinking outside the box, I put together a great pet first aid and medicine chest. My main suppliers were Tractor Supply Company (TSC), Dr. Foster and Smith (DFS), Lambert Vet Supply (LVS), Countryside Pet Supply (CPS) and Walgreens Pharmacy (WP).

I, of course, had all the usual things you would find in a human first aid kit such as gauze pads and bandages, tweezers, thermometer, bandage tape and scissors, but I had many other things as well. Included were my flea preventatives and dewormers as indicated in the previous chapters.

I set aside a cabinet just for it and kept everything there unless it had to be refrigerated. I made sure to have the phone number of my veterinarian as well as the emergency clinic posted on the cabinet door. Also included was the number to poison control.

SYRINGES

3 CC SYRINGES – These syringes are used for all vaccines, applying fipronil to larger dogs for flea prevention, fenbendazole for deworming, and many other medications. For large supplies of the syringes, I order from Lambert Vet Supply. For smaller supplies, these can be purchased in the livestock section of Tractor Supply.

TUBERCULIN 1CC SYRINGES – Sometimes confused with insulin syringes. They are not. These syringes are used to dose out most things UNDER 1 cc. That includes many medications as well as Ivomec for deworming and fipronil for fleas prevention on smaller animals. LVS or TSC

6 CC OR 12 CC SYRINGE – I always keep at least one or two of these syringes in case I need to administer large quantities of hydrogen peroxide or flush out a wound. LVS or TSC.

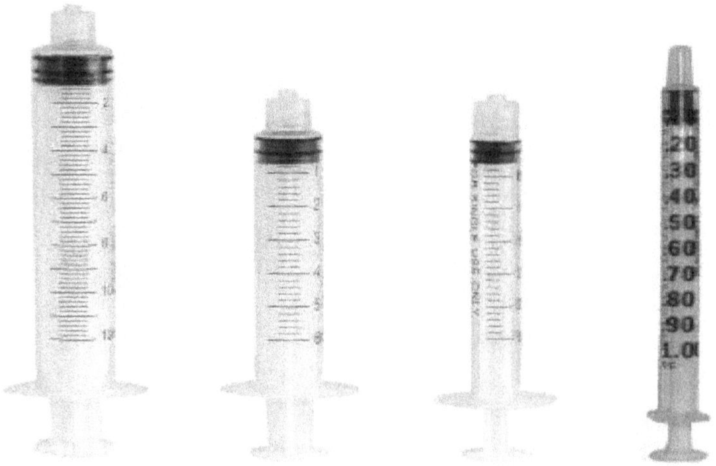

12 cc 6 cc 3 cc 1 cc

CREAMS, POWDERS, AND OINTMENTS

WONDERDUST – A blood coagulant and granulating agent for certain types of wounds. I have used it on hot spots before with success. Can also stop bleeding on a broken nail. A bottle costs between $6-10 and can be found in the equine department at TSC.

NITROFURAZONE/FURA-ZONE/NFZ PUFFER Topical antibiotic ointment that is effective against a wide variety of gram-negative and gram-positive organisms. It is particularly useful on burns. A small tub costs about $10 (TSC). NFZ is the powder form and makes it easier to apply for ear infections. It is also known to treat eye infections. (TSC) While the thoughts of a powder for eye infections is a bit uncomfortable, those who use it swear by its efficacy. If I were to have to choose only one, I would choose the Puffer.

PETROLEUM JELLY (Vaseline) – This comes in handy as a lubricant for a thermometer. It is also good to put on the ears of your dogs if fly bite is an issue as it will discourage the flies from biting. I often use it on dry, cracked dog elbows if they seem uncomfortable. (WP)

HYDROCORTISONE CREAM – Topical cream commonly sold for bug bites or itchy skin. My favorite is Cortizone 10 Brand. Works great on hot spots. Another option is Gold Bond Medicated Lotion in the green bottle. One winter, when our chihuahua was having a horrible time with his skin and losing fur, I covered him with Gold Bond, put a t-shirt on him so he couldn't lick it off and the relief was nearly instantaneous. His hair grew back quickly. (WP)

TRIPLE ANTIBIOTIC OINTMENT – Topical cream good for cuts and scrapes and can be used in the eyes if no other ointment is available. Look for Neosporin or Polysporin. (WP)

TERRAMYCIN – Broad Spectrum antibiotic cream to treat primary and secondary eye infections. (DFS) Apply twice daily.

CLOTRIMAZOLE – One of the main ingredient in the most prescribed ear infection drug, Otomax. Sold over the counter for humans as an athlete's foot treatment and feminine vaginal infection treatment. For pets, it is normally for treatment of yeast infections in the ear and can also be used for treatment of ringworm.

For eye infections

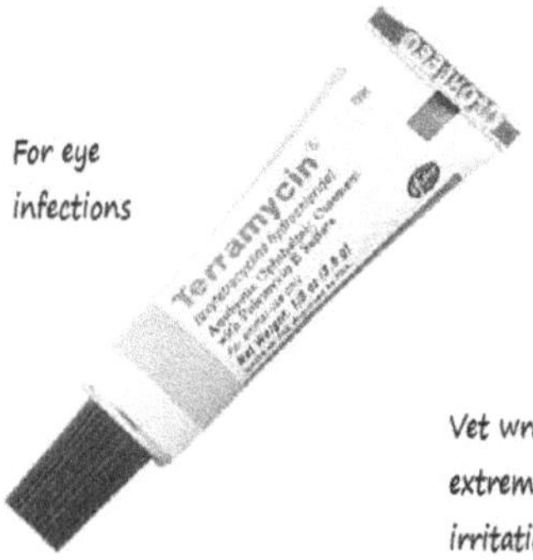

Vet wrap for bandaging injured extremities or covering certain skin irritations.

For yeast infections in ears or ringworm on skin. Same ingredient as in Otomax

Nitrofurazone for burns, skin infections, hot spots

NFZ puffer is nitrofurazone in powder form. For eye, ear, or skin infections.

Works as a coagulant to stop bleeding. Also good for skin wounds and hot spots.

ANTIBIOTICS

**Important note about antibiotics: Antibiotics should be prescribed by a vet for your pet. The reason for this is because people either don't know what to use, or use it improperly causing germs to build up a resistance to the medications. That being said, there have been times when I did not have the money to pay an office visit and buy the medications. Some vets even require your pet be vaccinated (even while ill) before they will treat the animal. So, in all honesty, I have treated my pets at home before, but only when I had no other choice.

There are several antibiotics that are sold for fish that are the same EXACT medication for dogs and cats. Since they are sold for fish, they are sold without a prescription. The best that I have found are made by Thomas Labs which is pharmacist owned, and sold at Lambert Vet Supply and Countryside Pet Supply, among others.

API is a company that sells fish supplies as well and can be found in most local pet stores in case there is no time to order online.

METRONIDAZOLE – sold as Fish Zole, (250 mg). In the human world, known as Flagyl. First choice of drug when the intestinal tract is involved. Also treats giardia. I rarely see this drug used in cats. For dogs, the dosage is 3mg to 23mg/lb. twice daily. My rule of thumb has always been under 25 lb. gets 1 capsule twice daily for 7 days. Over 25 lbs. gets 2 capsule twice daily for 7 days.

CEPHALEXIN- sold as Fish Flex (250mg) or Fish Flex Forte (500 mg), known to many as Keflex. This is a broad spectrum antibiotic used for skin infections, urinary tract infections, and many other infections. It is similar to Amoxicillin, (sold as Fish Flox), but it is not penicillin based and is my antibiotic of choice. Dosage is 10-15mg/lb. twice daily for 7 days. Again, my rule of thumb has always been under 25 lbs. gets 1 capsule twice daily, over 25 lbs. gets 2 capsules twice daily (or 1 500 mg twice daily).

CLINDAMYCIN – sold as Fish Cin (150 mg) Drug of choice for infections of the mouth. The usual dose for dogs is 2.5mg-15mg/lb. every 12 hours for a max of 28 days (usually 7-14 days). For cats dosage is 5mg-15mg/lb. once every 24 hours. This has such a wide dosage range, so I continue to use my under 25 lbs. = 1 capsule twice daily, over 25 lbs. = 2 capsules twice daily. For cats, I open the capsule, using the powder and put 1 capsule in canned food once daily.

CIPROFLOXACIN – sold as Fish Flox (R), comes in 250mg and 500 mg, strong antibiotic to treat infection of the skin, urinary tract and kidney, and respiratory system,2.27-6.8mg/pound every 12 hours. So about 70 mg per 10 lbs. of body weight.

KETACONAZOLE -Sold as Fish Fungus ® or in human form as Nizoral ® , Oral medication for treatment of yeast infection when other methods don't work. Often used for Cushings Disease as well. Never use with an animal taking cisapride. Dosage is 2.2-13 mg per pound for both dogs and cats every 12-24 hours.

There are many other antibiotics available including amoxicillin, ampicillin, tetracycline, erythromycin, terramycin, penicillin, and sulfamethoxazole /trimethoprim (SMZ-TMP). Although I didn't keep these stocked in my pet medicine chest, I kept them in mind as some could be used for my pocket pets as well, if needed.

Cephalexin (Keflex)

Clindamycin

Ketoconazole

SMZ-TMP

Metronidazole

OVER THE COUNTER SUPPLIES

HYDROGEN PEROXIDE – Peroxide's best use is to get a pet to vomit when he/she has ingested something harmful. It should not be done unless instructed by a vet or poison control to do so. This is what I keep a large 12 cc syringe for as it makes it easier to give. (WG)

ACTIVATED CHARCOAL GEL – Used as a first aid in case of accidental poisoning. Counteracts some toxic agents, but should be used only after contacting poison control or veterinarian. (TSC)

LAXATONE – Usually used as a hairball remedy. Works great as a gentle laxative and is okay for regular use. If your dog or cat has frequent problems with constipation add canned pumpkin to their food. (LVT) (CPS)

NUTRI-CAL – A high calorie nutritional supplement that is great for animals who aren't eating well. (LVS) (CPS)

KARO SYRUP – The same syrup you use on pancakes. Perfect to raise the blood sugar on an animal who hasn't eaten and is close to diabetic shock. For someone with chihuahuas, this is something I keep on hand since chihuahuas are known for having their blood sugar drop quickly when they don't eat.

DIPHENHYDRAMINE – Better known as Benadryl. Counteracts vaccine reactions and bee sting reactions and is great as a mild sedative. If I see my dog get stung by a bee, I immediately give Benadryl. If I have no other tranquilizer during a storm, for example, this works great. Often, for seasonal allergies (like we have), dogs will get itchy. This is great for that. Dosage for dogs is 1 mg per lb. of body weight. I buy the tablet form rather than capsule making it easier to break into for smaller dosages. (WG)

CHLORAPHENARAMINE – Also known as Chlor-Trimeton. An antihistamine similar to diphenhydramine, but it doesn't cause as much drowsiness. It tends to work on itchiness when Benadryl doesn't. I always give one tablet once to twice daily (WG)

LOPERAMIDE- Also known as Imodium ® 2mg. Treatment for diarrhea. Doesn't treat the reason for the diarrhea, but slows the motility. If the stool is bloody, the pet should see the vet asap. For dogs only. Dogs: 0.05-0.1 mg/pound by mouth every 8 hours. (WG)

FAMOTADINE – also known as Pepcid ® . Works great to reduce the stomach acid in dogs. 0.25mg/lb. of body weight every 12-24 hours (WG)

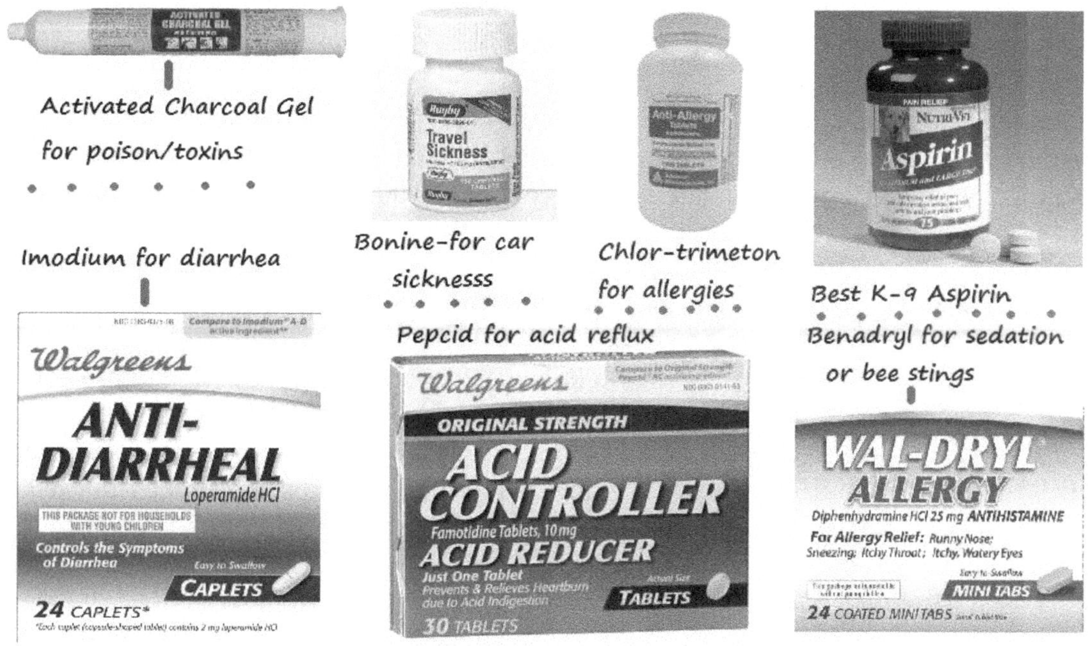

NUTRI-VET CANINE ASPIRIN Since dogs are so prone to stomach upset and bleeding with aspirin, you have to be careful with it. The great thing about this brand of aspirin is it is not only buffered for the pet, it is in a flavor that is easier to give. (DFS). If this is not available baby aspirin can be used, but do not give on an empty stomach. Dosage is 10 mg/lb. of body weight if using a baby or regular aspirin. As for pain control in cats, the simple answer is DON'T. Cats hide their pain very well. If a cat is showing you significant pain, drop everything you have and go to the vet. Its that serious. There are no safe over the counter remedies (and few prescription remedies) that a cat can metabolize. (DFS)

**Regarding pain medications: Never use the following in dogs or cats: Tylenol (Acetaminophen), Advil (Ibuprofen) or Aleve (Naproxen)

MECLIZINE – commonly known as Bonine ® Anti-Vert ® and Dramamine II ® (not the original). Works better than the original go-to drug for motion sickness because it is longer lasting and doesn't cause as much drowsiness. The dosage is one 25 mg tablet per day for dogs (not weight dependent) or 12.5 (or ½ a 25 mg tablet) per day for cats. Can also help with upset stomachs related to inner ear disease. (WC)

#10 SURGICAL BLADE – The same blade your vet uses. I keep several on hand for skin scraps or abscesses. The blades can be purchased at TSC as a “castration pack” in the livestock aisle.

LACTATED RINGERS & ADMINISTRATION SET – LRS or Lactated Ringers Solution is what is used in veterinary medicine for dehydration. Unlike in humans, fluids can be administered under the skin (subcutaneously or “sub-Q”). Although not as effective as providing fluids IV, it has helped save many animals from death. Can be purchased at your veterinarian or online at www.atlanticmedsupply.com. A 1000 ml bag of LRS is about $8.99 (a 250 ml bag is $6.99) and the IV administration set is $4.99. The shipping is a bit high, but better than not having it at all. Look for the Braun Basic IV Administration Set. I always use 18 gauge needles. Never give more than 100 ml in any one site.

THICK TOWEL OR CAT BAG- In order to hold a cat for treatment, you need to protect yourself from the nails as well as the teeth. You can do this using a thick towel or a cat bag. I am not a fan of cat bags. It stresses the cat out getting in it, and if the cat is upset already, good luck getting cooperation. However, once inside, it does hold the cat snug. I prefer to use a thick towel and make a “kitty burrito”.

As a vet tech, two things I always kept close, a thick towel, and a slip lead. (More on the slip lead later).

On the following page, you will see how to make a “kitty burrito”. It is the ideal way. Keep in mind, if a cat is already upset, and you need to grab it fast, its best to just throw the towel over the cat. Some technicians will grab an angry cat first by the “scruff” of the neck (as mother cats do), without remembering that two things can happen. One, the cat's back claws can still scratch your arm, and two, the cat can still flip over. I learned that the hard way.

Worse case scenario, and the cat is angry enough and you are in danger of getting hurt, let the cat go. You can both rest for a while and calm down and try again.

The making of a Kitty Burrito using a thick towel. The thicker the towel, the less the claws can scratch. On a bigger cat, hold the animal firmly behind the head with both hands while the pet is sternal (laying on tummy)

Never hold an adult cat like this. To maintain control, always keep the cat sternal on the table with the towel snug. Be prepared to add a little weight and hold the towel together to keep cat from escaping. Picture for demonstration purposes only.

As the cats rests sternally in the middle of the towel, wrap the left side as far to the right as possible, then wrap the right side to the left. Make it snug.

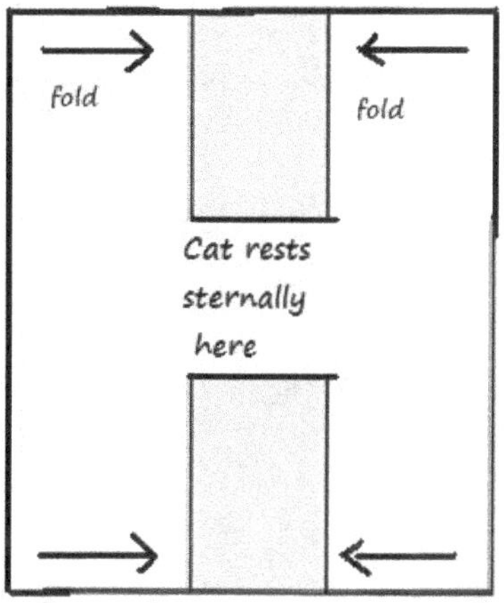

Allow the cat to have her head out of the towel. She can rest on your lap, but keep the towel snug, so she cannot escape.

SLIP LEADS-These are the leashes you see used at vet offices. They are one piece leashes with a ringlet on one end that turns it into a soft choke collar. They are vital to the life of a technician and have saved me from getting scratched, bitten, and otherwise inconvenienced many times. They allow better control than conventional leashes and collars together. Normally, when holding a dog with a slip lead, they want to get away from you. Only once in my entire career have I had a dog come toward me and try to attack. I learned after that, never to allow myself to get too comfortable.

Slip leads can be used to make a quick muzzle by slipping it over the muzzle, tightening quickly, and wrapping it around the end around the muzzle several times. Its not my favorite, but in a pinch, it does wonders.

They can even be used to make a harness to bathe a cat (choke collars should never be used on cats). Below is a diagram describing how to make a harness. Sometimes, if using the 4 ft. rather than 6 ft. slip leads, you may have to use two 4 ft. leads to give you enough to tie to a solid object. I often tie to the faucet base if nothing else is available. This method allows cats to get angry if they want, but makes sure that they don't get away and that they don't choke. It also helps to let them stand on a milk crate (if there is room in the sink). They feel safer having something that isn't slippery to stand on. A cat that feels safe, is a happier cat, and will make bathing much easier.

Creating the harness is a two step process.

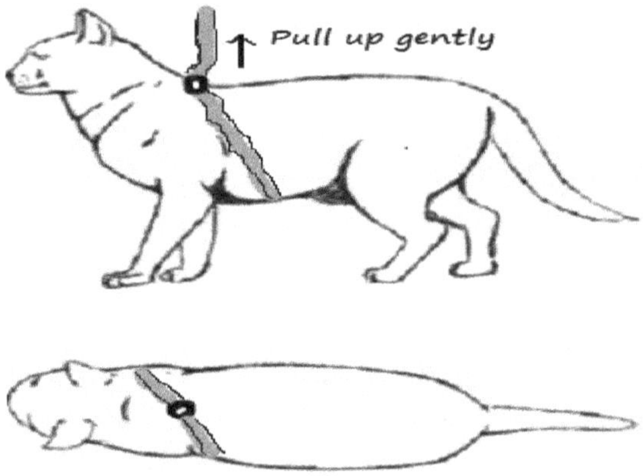

STEP ONE:
To make a cat harness, use a slip lead which is simply a one piece leash you see used in vet offices. Fit the leash over the head as you would with a dog, however instead of tightening it around the neck, put one end under one leg, leaving the other up towards the shoulder, and pull up gently.

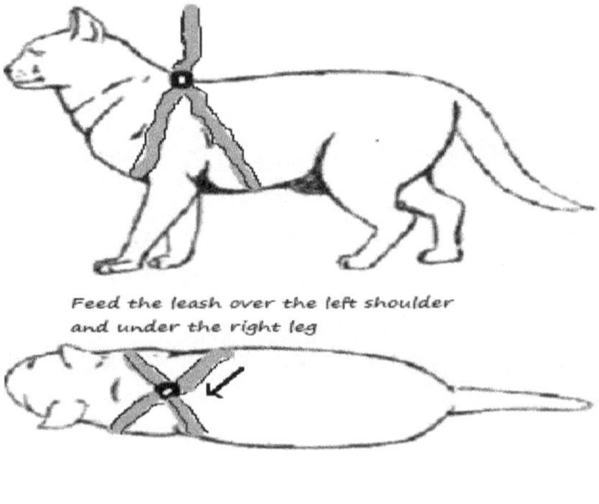

Step 2
Take the portion of the leash that you have just pull up on, and feed it over the opposite shoulder (in this case the left shoulder), under the opposite leg (the right) and feed it through the ringlet pulling up again. You now have a harness. It is important to keep it snug, however, with the harness, the cat can be bathed or treated without choking.

HOMEMADE AND COST CUTTING SOLUTIONS

You will notice that most of my homemade solutions are kept in squeeze bottles. I tend to buy these in bulk. You can buy them from craft and kitchen stores as well as Ebay and Amazon. Buy different sizes. The great thing about them, is, if you need to use a syringe, you simply cut the tip to the correct size and you have no mess. I love them.

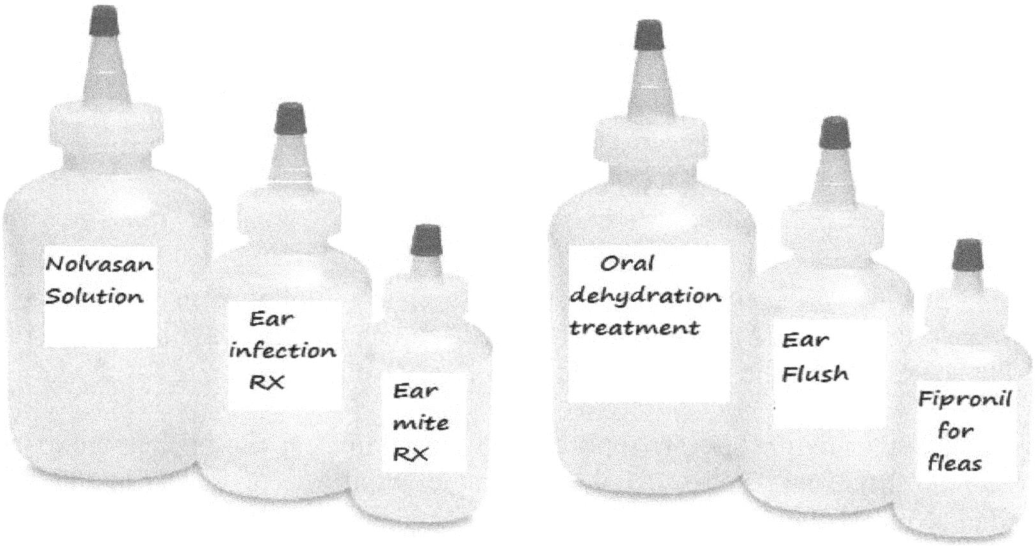

NOLVASAN SOLUTION – Used for cleaning wounds and flushing out abscesses. 1:2 ratio

- ½ cup Nolvasan
- 1 cup warm water

Mix well and use as appropriate. Will not burn.

ORAL DEHYDRATION TREATMENT – To give orally if pet is dehydrated but not vomiting. If vomiting, pet will need subcutaneous fluids.

- 1 cup beef/chicken/pork bullion
- 1 cup hot water
- 1 packet ReSorb ®

Mix bouillon cube in 1 cup hot water until dissolved. Put contents in pitcher. Add enough water to make 2 quarts. Add entire contents of Resorb (both sides of packet) and stir. Allow to cool a little and serve. Refrigerate remaining. Best to serve warm.

EAR CLEANING SOLUTION- use as often as needed. Helps keep an acidic environment in the ear which prevents infections Ratio 1:2

- ½ Apple Cider Vinegar
- 1 cup warm water

Mix well and use as necessary, but at least once weekly. If treating an ear infection use one to two times daily.

EAR MITE TREATMENT: (similar to Acaraxx 0.01% ivomectin)

- 1.2 ml Ivomec 1% injection for cattle and swine
- 118.8 ml of warm water

You will need a measuring cup and a 3 ml syringe. Pull up 1.2 ml of Ivomec. Add the ivomec to the measuring cup first. Add warm water to the ½ cup mark. This will be 118.8 ml of warm water. Put contents in plastic squeeze bottle. Shake very well.

Draw up 1cc of the mixture per ear. Apply to each ear holding ear closed once applied. The cat will attempt to shake, but it is best to hold closed at least thirty seconds. The application should not need to be repeated unless the cat is an outdoor cat that becomes reinfested. You can dispose of the remaining liquid or keep for future use.

EAR INFECTION TREATMENT (for bacterial and yeast infections) Ratio 1:1:1

- 1 tbsp nitrofurazone (for example)
- 1 tbsp clotrimazole
- 1 tbsp hydrocortisone cream

Mix thoroughly. Put in an appropriate sized squeeze bottle. You may need to clip the tip off the bottle for the medication to come through. The nozzle on the bottle will allow you to put the medication far down into the ear canal. Repeat twice daily for 10-14 days. Clean ears at least once daily with vinegar water ear cleaning solution.

HOMEMADE DOG AND CAT SHAMPOO – using an empty one gallon container (like a water or milk jug), follow this recipe:

- 1 cup Apple Cider Vinegar (must be apple cider)
- 1 cup Dawn Dishwashing Liquid (only the original)
- 1 packet Aveeno Oatmeal Bath Treatment
- Add warm water to top and shake.

CHAPTER 11

WHERE TO CONCENTRATE YOUR VET DOLLARS

I realize there are probably quite a few people appalled at all I have done for my animals at home. If I was a good pet owner, they would say, I would have my animals taken care of properly at the vet. To that I would say there is a perfect world, and then there is reality. You do the best you can. So, what I can do at home, I do. Then I save the money to do the most important stuff.

PROFESSIONAL DENTAL CLEANINGS
One of the keys I believe, to your pet living a long life, is taking care of his/her teeth.

You have to consider that most of us brush our teeth at least once daily. Most dogs and cats do not get that. Tartar and calculus builds up, gingivitis kicks in, the gums get inflamed and eventually infected. There are things I have seen in the mouth of pets as a veterinary technician that are so disgusting, that I wouldn't put the photograph in this book. Most of the times, those animals, are companions to some very good people who just did not look inside their dog or cat's mouth.

All the bacteria that is in the mouth and oral cavity, find its way into the bloodstream and through the body causing illness. It can destroy the kidneys and the heart. Dental cleanings are not just to keep Fido's breath nice and fresh. They prolong Fido's life.

I'm a firm believer that dogs and cats should eat primarily dry food in order to have a healthy mouth. While one can flavor the kibble with canned food, the kibble serves to remove the tarter as the pet eats.

You can brush their teeth at home, but with the number of pets I have, I would never do anything else. To do a good job, they need to be sedated. So I check their teeth frequently and try to afford to have one or two done a year. I have been surprised how well some of them have aged without having too many issues. Mr. Buster, my basset mix, has the cleanest teeth of the bunch and he is over ten years old. Some breeds just have more problems than others.

You have to keep in mind that animals have an instinct not to show pain. This is particularly true in cats. Dogs and cats will eat with a bad tooth until they can't take it any longer. This is why it is our responsibility to check their teeth and gums frequently.

One of the best ways to save money on professional dental cleanings is to do them in February, which is always Pet Dental Cleaning Month. Many clinics will offer significant discounts during this month. Call around and see who is giving the best deal. Always be sure to ask what is included in the price. Some will include pre-anesthetic lab work. If you let them know your budget is tight, some will even help you find ways to save such as bringing the pet in a few days early to send the blood work out instead of doing it in house which is typically more expensive. Also ask if there are any other costs. Some will require that you have your pet fully vaccinated and will not recognize any you have done yourself. Another additional cost might be extractions. Be prepared ahead of time.

LAB TESTING AS THE VOICE FOR YOUR PET

I'm a firm believer that you do everything you can yourself, but be able to acknowledge when you need help. As much as I can know my animal, they cannot voice how they feel. They can whimper and cry, but they can't say "my tummy hurts". I can see if they are showing tenderness there, but I can't see inside.

There are two things in veterinary medicine that acts as the voice of the animal. One is an x-ray and/or ultrasound, and the other is blood and laboratory testing. I most certainly cannot do an x-ray or an ultrasound at home. And even though I have taken hundreds of x-rays over my career and assisted in many ultrasound, I admit, I cannot read them like a veterinarian can. So I must admit my limit.

In addition, I cannot do more specific laboratory tests such as a complete blood panel, chemistries, thyroid levels, or urine cultures. These are very thorough tests, that although, expensive (~$50-$175+), sometimes they are the only way to properly diagnose a pet. When a vet tells me it is necessary to do these tests, I do everything in my power to do it.

UNDERSTANDING A RADIOGRAPH (X-RAY)

While an x ray may be self-explanatory, there are a few things it helps to understand. First, radiography for pets has come a long way in recent years. Now that digital films are available, the images are crisper, clearer, and the veterinarian can adjust the film on the computer to make it lighter, darker, and even magnified to get the best view possible.

For people stretching their budget to afford an x-ray, this is a good thing since you really want as few films as possible done. However, even with all this advancement one view (picture) rarely is enough. Let me explain why. With an x-ray, you are looking at a three dimensional object on a two dimensional film. It's like looking at a Polaroid thinking the guy in the picture is Uncle Bob, but you turn around to say high and see his profile, and you realize you don't even know him. That's where the terms "lateral" and "v/d" (or d/v) come in.

Typically, when taking an x-ray of the abdomen, for instance, you lay the dog resting on his/her side (normally right side down). That's called a lateral view. The results of that view may show a little area of abnormality (could it be Uncle Bob?), but you can't be sure. So you lay the pet either on his/her back (v/d) or less commonly, on his/her abdomen (d/v) and take another view.

The veterinarian puts those two images together in her mind, compares them, and realizes that either:

1)everything looks normal
2) things appear abnormal and medication can be prescribed
3)things appear abnormal and further study needs to rule out an obstruction, or torsion

You have to keep in mind that certain things cannot be seen in a typical x-ray. No matter how good the technician, if Fido eats your socks, the chances of her seeing the Nike ® logo on them are slim. Most soft objects cannot be seen in an x ray unless they contain some type of metal. Normally, the only thing a typical x-ray will indicate is that the food you told them Fido ate 12 hours ago is still in his stomach. That's very important information and the best starting point. Then it's time for some barium.

Barium is a liquid that can be seen on an x-ray. Barium series radiographs work on a time lapse. Fido is given barium usually by using a syringe and some encouragement. Depending on the vet instructions, at least one lateral film will be taken every 15-30 minutes. If the barium passes through the stomach, small and large intestine, and colon, a foreign body can usually be ruled out. However, it stops, Fido needs surgery immediately.

UNDERSTANDING A CBC

In order to understand the importance of these tests, it helps to put them into simpler terms. While the values (number) are different depending on species, these are the same tests your own doctor performs when trying to understand what is making you sick.

The results can be overwhelming. They are big words that mean nothing to you with numbers that mean even less. A CBC or complete blood panel, for instance. What does that even mean? Let me simplify it a bit. It will help you understand why it is so important for the veterinarian to do it.

There are three basic parts of the blood. The test looks at the levels of all three including: white blood cells (WBC), called leukocytes as well as red blood cells (RBC), and Platelets.

WBC are important for fighting off infection. If you have a high WBC count, there is a very good chance there is a bacterial infection somewhere. There are different types of WBC that are in charge of different things. The number of each can show a vet a little more detail. For instance if the monocytes are increased, the infection may be caused by an allergic reaction to something.

RBC counts tell you all about how many red blood cells are in the body which is really important because they are in charge of getting oxygen throughout the body and carbon dioxide out. If the count is low, you are anemic and your body is having difficulty getting oxygen. However, it's not good for it to be too high either because too many RBC can block the oxygen from getting through to the rest of the body. There are other values within a RBC count that tell you specifics such as how dense the RBC count number is, and how good of a job the RBC's are doing of carrying the oxygen.

Platelets are in charge of blood clotting. Too few and you can't stop bleeding. Too many, and you can have a blood clot.

UNDERSTANDING A CHEMISTRY PROFILE

Blood chemistry tests are often called internal organ profiles (IOP). The results of these tell you how well each organ is working. While some wish to be able to focus on one organ (say a kidney, when there seems to be a urine problem), keep in mind that one organ affects another. That's why it's best to perform all at once. And generally, it's not much more expensive to do so. By organ, here is what each test analyzes.

LIVER: Alkaline Phosphatase, ALT (SGPT), Total Bilirubin, Cholesterol
KIDNEY: BUN, Creatinine
PANCREAS : Blood Glucose, Lipase, Amylase
ELECTROLYTES: Sodium, Potassium, Chloride, Magnesium
PROTEINS: Albumin, Total Protein, Globulin

I would be remiss in saying if a BUN value, for example, is this number (fill in the blank), then your pet is in kidney failure. Reading a CBC and chemistry is an art unto itself. Veterinarians are taught to read the big picture. This is why I say I must acknowledge that this is something I cannot do myself. While I performed hundreds of these tests in my career, I still do not have the skill it takes to read the tests with the same skill a veterinarian has. I can't tell you how many times I have taken the results of an IOP to the on call vet expecting bad news only to hear "Ok, not bad." So, I can guarantee you, taking the results of your pet's lab work home, getting on the internet and trying to translate the values, will only serve to scare you or confuse you. Trust your vet's interpretation.

UNDERSTANDING A THYROID TEST

I mention a thyroid test, because thyroid issues are becoming more and more common it seems in dogs and cats. The thyroid glands are responsible for the metabolism along with other functions. It can be too low (hypothyroidism) or too high (hyperthyroidism). There are a number of tests that evaluate its function. The most common is the T4. If it indicates an issue, further testing should be done.

Many people do not realize the effects of a low or high thyroid. For instance, with low thyroid (hypothyroidism) the following symptoms may occur: lethargy, weight gain (with no increase in appetite), hair loss, dull coat, chronic itchy skin, dry skin, frequent skin infections, cold temperature intolerance, slow heart rate, frequent ear infections, behavioral changes, depression.

High thyroid (hyperthyroidism) symptoms are: weight loss (with increase in appetite), restlessness and hyperactivity, increased heart rate, increase in frequency of defecation and size of stools, increase in thirst and urination, matting of the fur with a greasy coat, reddening of the mucous membranes.

Although thyroid tests are not cheap, in the long run they can save you money. You may return over and over to the vet or to the pet store looking for something for chronic itchy skin when you could have had this test, confirmed hypothyroidism, and had the pet on thyroxine. By bringing the thyroid levels into balance, you took care of many problems with one pill.

I share this information with you to help you understand why the CBC, blood chemistry profiles, thyroid panels, and x-rays can be the voice for your pet and why they are worth the cost. Most of this book has explained how to save money so when the time comes and your pet needs these procedures, you will have the necessary resources for them.

HOW TO FINANCE THE PROCEDURES

Care Credit ® is a healthcare credit card that is good, not only for pet's, but people too. It allows a particular amount of time interest-free to repay what you owe. That way, you are prepared for emergencies and can afford this test when you need them.

A Pet Saving Account is also an option. While, difficult for many of us to save, one thing I do is save all my change. I keep a bucket near where I empty my pockets and put all my change there. It adds up over time. At times, it has helped me buy food for my animals when times were tough.

One thing I have done many times is sell on Ebay, Craigslist, and Amazon. I have found there are many things around the house I don't need. I've also mentioned to my friends that I am raising money and they have brought over things for me to sell. Sometimes I will just have a yard sale and put it in savings toward pet bills.

There are also some websites that will help you create an online fundraiser that you can tell your Facebook friends about. Give Forward.com helps you set up your own online fundraiser for a small fee.

For emergencies, there is at least one online organization that can help. IMOM.org allows you to apply for financial aid. This is for emergencies only, however.

The Pet Medication Drug Card is similar to human drug cards that you can get a local pharmacies. It provides savings up to 75% at participating pharmacies and can be applied for at www.petmedicationcard.com.

The HSUS provides links by state and breed. It is a great resource to begin your search for financial assistance. Go to:
http://www.humanesociety.org/animals/resources/tips/trouble_affording_veterinary_care.htm

RULES AND SECRETS FOR AN ECONOMICAL & SUCCESSFUL VET VISIT
You are sitting in the exam room and the veterinarian or his/her assistant has just gone over the estimate for treatment with you. You love your pet with all your heart, but you are thinking as hard as you can how you can afford treatment and still be able to pay the bills or even get groceries. What do you do? Here is how to make sure the visit goes as well as possible and in your pet's favor:

- RULE #1: Be honest with them and don't get a bad attitude. Until proven otherwise, they have your pet's best interest at heart. Be respectful to the staff. If your pet has been sick all day and you wait until 5:30 to show up for an exam, that is not showing respect. And do not talk on the phone when the vet or technician is trying to speak with you. If you need to speak to a family member regarding the situation, ask for a few minutes alone.
- RULE #2: Bring all the records you have on the pet. The more the vet knows of the history, the better. Even if you are going to your regular vet, you may be referred to a specialist or to an emergency clinic and they will need that information.
- RULE #3: Ask them to go over the absolute necessities and if there are any options. Is it cheaper to send the blood work out to another lab then do it in house for instance? If they suspect your pet may be diabetic, is it cheaper to do a simple urine strip test first? Instead of doing all the lab tests at once, (x-rays, cbc, iof), can they do the most important first to see if that will tell them what they need to know? If they do an x ray and see a Tonka Truck in the tummy of your dog, they are pretty well sure, that is the issue.
- RULE #4: Don't be afraid to ask questions. Most vets and their assistants honestly want to help you. They should be able to explain the value of their treatment plan. If the person presenting the estimate cannot answer your questions, ask for someone else.
- RULE #5: Take your phone with you if possible. If you have an internet capable smart phone even better. If you do find yourself at an office that is giving you a bad attitude, or whose prices are far beyond anything you can consider, remember they are not the only

vet in the area. However, assume they are really trying to help until they prove differently. Never be the first one with a bad attitude.

- RULE #6: Know that prices vary greatly depending on location and if the office is part of a national chain. In national chains, such as those found inside of big box pet stores, those veterinarians have no say in price. A small privately owned vet hospital may not have the buying power of a national chain, but they have the advantage of autonomy and being able to make their own decisions. It doesn't hurt to call another vet and make an appointment for a second opinion. Most vet hospitals will not give prices of services (beyond an office visit), so price shopping isn't always easy. However, it never hurts to ask. Another possibility is to check with local vet schools. Many times they will see your pet at a discount to give their students experience.
- RULE #7: Take advantage of competition. Until a few years ago, the only place you could purchase your pet's medication, was through the same doctor who was prescribing it. The markup was significant and often included a "prescription filling fee" of $6-10. That is what you paid for the technician to count the tablets. Now, there is much greater competition because of companies like 1800 Pet Meds. Another advantage to having an internet capable smart phone is being able to look up the price and see if the vet will be willing to match it. Many vets will. Now, even more to the advantage of pet parents, is the national human pharmacy involvement. Since many of the same medications used for pets are also used for humans, pharmacies can sell you that generic medication Fluffy needs for around $4, the same price you would pay for your generic medication. Most pharmacies now have handouts that you can take with you showing all the medications they can fill for you. Keep that list with you and ask for a prescription to be written.
- RULE #8: If the vet prescribes a medication that is out of your reach, ask if there are any other options. Since the vet industry is having to change, (now that they cannot rely on markups of common medications), many will stock pet-only medications. In other words, medications made only for use in pets and not in humans. The advantage for them is that some of those may not be available at local pharmacies. It is actually a wise choice for the veterinarian, but can also mean that you cannot afford to treat your pet. If a good and caring vet realizes that, he/she will be more than willing to help you find an alternative. However, don't assume that there is always an alternative. There may not be.
- RULE #9: Follow your instincts. If you don't feel good about the veterinarian, vet techs, or the environment in general, go somewhere else. For instance, if you are told that your sick pet needs vaccinations while ill, a red flag should go up. This is especially true of elderly pets. If your pet is sick enough for expensive medical treatment, he/she is too sick for vaccines. Also keep in mind that when your pet goes to the treatment or hospital area, you need to be able to trust the people handling your pet. You also need to be assured it is a clean environment. Ask to be able to see the area where your pet will be treated and hospitalized. If they refuse, or if you feel uncomfortable, go to another hospital. Do keep in mind that a busy hospital at 11 am in the morning is not going to be

spotless, but they should be clean within reason.

- RULE #10: If your pet is sick enough that you must consider euthanasia, it helps to understand a few things. (IMPORTANT NOTE: While I am going to be very direct about the practicalities of this procedure in this chapter, I will help you understand the more emotional aspect later.)

The cost for euthanasia varies. Some humane societies will offer it for free while some clinics will charge hundreds. Make phone calls if you cannot afford the price given you by your vet. Often the difference is because a veterinary clinic might require an IV catheter be installed prior to the euthanasia. There are a few reasons for this. One, if the pet has been ill, his/her blood pressure may be very low. This can make finding a vein necessary to inject the euthanasia solution very difficult. The solution itself is thick, and it can collapse the vein. So there are times when it is appropriate.

I have to admit, it does bother me, however, when an animal with a perfectly good vein is forced to have an IV catheter installed. Not only do I believe it is a waste of money, but I believe it is unnecessary pain for the pet. If I, as a technician, can perform the procedure easily without an IV catheter, then the veterinarian should have no problem.

I am equally frustrated when cats are forced to have a catheter, particularly those with very little blood pressure. As I will discuss in a later chapter, intraperitoneal (IP) euthanasia is by far the most peaceful procedure taught by the American Humane Association. IP is done by injecting the euthanasia solution into a certain part of the abdomen. It cannot be done using certain combination solutions and under certain circumstances (like during pregnancy), but when your sick cat can fall asleep purring in your arms as she passes on, it is worth having your vet look into it. The reason, I believe, most veterinarians do not use this procedure is that it takes longer for the pet to pass away (an average of seven minutes compared to seconds), and it requires three times the amount of solution compared to performing it by IV. I believe that the peaceful and pain free aspect is worth every moment and every dime.

When I am looking for a veterinarian to call my fur family doctor, one of the things I ask is if they are willing to look into IP euthanasia for my cats. If they are, I give them this website information:
http://www.americanhumane.org/animals/professional-resources/training/euthanasia-by-injection.html

It is not unheard of for veterinarians and/or veterinary staff to have never gone through proper euthanasia training. I had worked in hospitals for years before attending my certification course and I learned an astounding amount of information that made the procedure so much easier for the pet and the family.

I realize that this section of the book is difficult to read, but I believe it is vital in being prepared and being able to afford to take proper care of your pet.

Depending on where you live, there are a few different options in what to do with the body. Your vet will be familiar with the legal aspects of your area. Some of the options include: 1) burying at home 2) vet disposal 3) cremation 4) pet cemetery 5) donating to science.

As I said, most jurisdictions will not allow at home burial, but if they do, it is a good alternative. I have to admit, for me, digging the grave has been part of the process of healing and letting go. Another alternative is to allow the vet to take care of the remains. There is a charge for this as the vet must pay the company who takes care of that. Cremation is another alternative. The pet is sent to a company who returns the cremated remains in a about a week. Normally, you can have this service done much cheaper if you deal directly with the cremation company instead of going through the veterinarian. Some of the cremation companies will also have a pet cemetery that are well cared for, but this is much more expensive. The final option, which is not easy to find, is to donate the pet to science. While living in Southern California, a local vet school, who did not want to take animals out of shelters for study, would pick up your deceased pet, and their students would learn from animals that were already deceased. When they had learned all they could, they had them cremated and returned, at no cost to you. To be honest, this was my favorite solution. My pets, whose spirits had already left their bodies, were preventing the death of another and helping to improve the care of the next generation.

CHAPTER 12

AGING AND LETTING GO

In my view, the only negative aspect of being loved by a pet is knowing that someday, I will have to let them go. Most of our pets, depending on species, live only a decade or so. For some people, the idea of facing that grief is too much to bear, so they don't allow themselves the immense joy of being a pet parent. I understand. I never thought I would get over the death of my precious Pepper, who choked. I never thought I could survive the passing of my best friend, Cuddles, who had been with me most of my adolescence. But I did. I realized that the weight of the grief was far outweighed by the love and the joy. The advantage in being a species that has an average lifespan of many decades, is there is more time to love more. For me, as one passes, another comes my way who needs me, and whose love fills my heart and helps me heal from my grief.

As with humans, with age in our pets, come health issues. Arthritis, incontinence, diabetes, hormonal problems, hearing and eyesight deficiencies, mental and cognitive issues, and more. Animals adjust so much better than we do for the most part. Often, a pet parent will not even notice that their pet has gone blind until they move the furniture. Or, he/she will think their dog is simply being stubborn when they just can't hear them. It is up to us to realize that we must adjust our way of thinking as the pet ages. We need to learn what their limits are and vow not to overdo it. While you may have only aged 10 years and can still run 10 miles, Fido has gone from a young pup, to an elderly dog.

Being mindful of frequent home physical exams comes even more important now. It is so easy for things to happen over time and, since you see your pet daily, you may not notice the significance of those changes. Cats, for instance, who have certain thyroid issues or even diabetes, will drop weight even though they have a ferocious appetite. Their fur will look dry and brittle. It may not occur to you how bad this issue is because it has happened over time. But if you do a weekly physical, you will notice the dehydration “tent” test reveals a problem. You might notice that the backbone and ribs are starting to stick out.

You are your pet's best chance of living a long healthy, comfortable life. The more you know about your pet, the better. When you know what is normal, you will notice what is abnormal quicker. Educate yourself on what you can do, and learn what you need to accept. For instance, for your blind pet, you can keep the environment and routine consistent. You can keep his eyes clean of debris, well lubricated, and comfortable. But you can't bring his/her sight back. And you MUST keep the well being of the pet first.

I experienced this personally with my dog, Duffy. Duffy was the son of Cuddles and Angel, my childhood dogs. Duffy was so full of life. Even as he aged, you would still think he was a puppy. He had moved with me from Virginia, to Tennessee, to New Orleans, and on to California. In New Orleans, he had injured his back severely and I thought he would never walk again, but he did. He was naughty in that he loved to tease the cats.

Being a Pekingese mix, his eyes were not well protected. I never was certain what caused it, but Duffy went blind. It was fast. There was no gradual changes. Just one day it was. I found him shaking in the corner. I could tell, his eyes were not focusing. The vet I worked for confirmed his blindness, but had no explanation. I hoped that he would adjust as most dogs do. But he didn't. He lived in constant fear that he could not see.

His body was still strong. He was all muscle. His organs worked fine. His lab work was superb. But his quality of life was gone. His spirit was broken. I had a decision to make. It wasn't an easy decision and it was not a fast one. I exhausted all possible solutions. The question I had to ask myself was, "Did I loved Duffy enough to stop his terror?" Yes, I could have kept his sedated constantly, but what kind of life was that? Was it one I would want to live? I am a very firm believer that one's QUALITY of life is much more important than QUANTITY. So at 14 years old, I let Duffy go. He went quietly and was free from his fears.

As a person now living in poverty, a very sad reality I have to accept is there are times when I may not be able to afford treatment for a long term illness. I've got to be very honest and tough in regards to this issue, so please have patience and let me give you an example.

A cat with diabetes has three options. One, you can treat him/her. To do so will require a few days to a week in the hospital in order to find the appropriate dose of insulin needed to regulate him/her. There will be multiple blood draws, multiple glucose tests to run, and a change in diet. Once the cat finally makes it home, there will be new prescription food to purchase, insulin and insulin syringes to buy. Someone will have to give the injections twice daily. A routine will have to be followed. More vet visits will be needed in order to continue to regulate the medication properly. That's option one.

Option two is do nothing. The cat will continue to lose weight rapidly in spite of eating. Ketones will build up in the system that will make him/her feel extremely sick. The organs will start to fail. The appetite will cease and the cat will become more and more dehydrated. Death will be slow and uncomfortable.

Option three, if you have no possible way to afford the treatment of the pet, is to be strong enough to admit it, and compassionate enough to give the pet who has loved you and whom you have loved, a gentle, quick release from illness.

Believe me, I know how much guilt runs through you when you think about euthanasia, particularly if the decision has to be made over money. If you have exhausted all other options, then the decision needs to be made. No one wants to be in that situation. If I could take that decision away from every one, I would, but the fact of the matter is, things happen. Ignoring the decision is really not ignoring it. Its saying “I chose to let my pet suffer so I don't have to make this decision”.

I know that is difficult to hear, but it happens far too commonly. I have seen animals die in horrible, horrible ways because their pet parents wanted to pretend nothing was happening. So while they stayed home trying to occupy themselves with something else, I held their dog while they struggled to breathe in terror until they died. It is not fair to the pet, and it is not fair to the veterinary staff.

The reality of euthanasia, is, it is a peaceful process. It is different from the days when my parents were young. The methods are far improved and the training better. I was trained by The American Humane Association. Most of the time, it is a veterinarian who performs the actual injection. In my case, because I was certified and worked at a humane society-operated clinic, I and one other technician, performed the entire process under the indirect supervision of the veterinarian.

Emotionally, it is not an easy thing to do, but knowing that you are providing that animal a final act of gentle kindness, helps you go on. My training had shown me ways of making it a very peaceful experience. I don't recall a single animal that struggled. In fact, using techniques that seem to be unique to the American Humane Association (the IP method mentioned earlier), pet parents were able to hold their cats, unafraid, as they drifted off to sleep and passed away peacefully. Many times I found comfort myself as the cat purred until near the end and the pet parent let go of their fears.

I share this to show you that euthanasia does not have to be an evil, fearful thing. I personally think we are blessed to have this option. While I have had to watch my elderly human family suffer tremendously while waiting to pass on, I have the option to give my pet a gentle transition to what lays beyond.

People ask me “How do you know the time is right?” No time feels good. Keeping the best interest of the pet first is very important. Although your heart is hurting, that pet is suffering. When he/she no longer eats or drinks, no longer finds joy in life, no longer shows interest in anything, it’s time to let go. For me, I believe their souls go on to better things and I take comfort in that.

CHAPTER 13

ALL THE OTHER DETAILS

So far, I have covered mostly the medical issues I have had to deal with over the years as a technician and rescuer. However, there are still many other practical things to consider.

KEEPING THE PEACE
One of the most important things was learning how to keep the peace.

Putting these animals together, with their various histories of abuse and neglect, had potential for disaster. The dogs varied from a 2 lb. chihuahua to a 50 lb. basset hound. Some were old, some were young. Others tended to be more alpha dogs, while others simply were happy being in the pack. A few liked people, while most were afraid of them.

While my guys loved jumping in a "puppy pile", there were times when they needed some alone time. I had crate trained them all for this very purpose. Dogs need a place to feel safe and call their own. Even when my dogs stay outside in the summer, I put their crates on the patio. If I look out the window, they are often asleep with 4-5 dogs to a cage with the door open.

However, if they get too excited, or get mad at each other, telling everyone to "kennel up" put a stop to it, and they all headed for their cages. Contrary to popular belief, being kenneled is not a punishment. It is like going home and laying down on your favorite couch.

I also made sure there were separate play areas. Some days, just like with people, your family gets on your nerves. There were days, Buster, the older basset hound, just needed a break from the younger ones. Other days, Panda, the pomeranian, could be so hyper, he could irritate a saint. And when the world was big and scary and a thunderstorm came, everyone wanted to f ind a safe place. So three separate areas were available when needed.

At feeding time, every dog was crated to keep the peace. I fed once daily, in the evenings. As soon as everyone was finished, the bowls were taken up and washed. Nothing was left behind to argue about. If anyone did get a little obnoxious, I kept a water bottle handy to spray to remind them I was there and not happy with their behavior.

I also tried to give everyone a job. Dogs loved to have a purpose. Teddy, was the big brother to all the foster dogs. He took his job very seriously. Casey, the biggest dog, slept just outside my bedroom door to make sure the rest of the house was protected. Buster, was in charge of keeping everyone in line. Tinker, took care of the non-canine pets. Blue, Panda, and Bojangles all monitored the fence line. Ms. Ruby took care of me, and was in charge of training Ms Pearl, the tiniest chihuahua, knew the ways of the Farris world, in case she needed to take over some day.

Routine is very important to dogs. The best way to keep them potty trained, eating correctly, and completely content, is to give them a routine. They like to know when to expect supper, when you are coming home from work, what time you are going to take him/her for a walk, and more.

I have to admit, there was one little trick that did help us bond. And I could only do it because I lived in a single family home away from neighbors. If life was particularly rough, for instance, thunderstorms that stressed them out, or fireworks on the 4th of July, I brought everyone inside for a few minutes, and we did a family howl. As embarrassing as it is, I just had to start the song "Delta Dawn", and immediately, the howling began. I joined in, and kept it going until every single dog had let out their best howl. As soon as we stopped, I always ended up laughing, they jumped up and down, and treats were passed around to everybody. The stress was gone, and everyone rested. Worked like a charm.

And although these behavioral things did wonders to make things work peacefully, I have to honestly say, some days I just sat down in the yard, gathered them around me, and talked to them. When I worried about money to buy food, they sat close while I cried. They took care of me for a while and it made us a family.

The same could be said for the cats. If I was overwhelmed, and being swarmed by a double-digit number of dogs were more than I could take, I would go sit under a shade tree in the side yard. No matter where the cats were on the property, somehow they knew, and everyone would gather around me. I was never left alone to deal with the world. I always had back up.

I knew that I must be doing something right the day one of the gates was left unlocked. Every dog I had could have left while I was gone, or, at the very least, chase the cats. There was a wooded area up the hill to explore and open fields to run in. There were neighborhood dogs to visit. Places to go, and new people to see. When I pulled in the driveway, one dog came running up to me, letting me know the gate was open, and I panicked. We both ran to the gate, and waiting patiently for me to return, was the entire canine family. They loved their home.

BEDDING AND HOUSING

So, for this wonderful family, I had a lot of details to attend to. One was bedding. Not only were we limited in funds, but there were numerous pets to provide for, and dogs who loved to rip up pillows.

As I mentioned, there were several areas for them to choose from. The large dog building, the stacked kennels on the patio, the dog houses scattered throughout their space. And for the cats, they had their cat building, a garage, and some of their favorite places, under dense shrubbery. In the summer, it was simple. Friends gave me their old sheets to put in their crates which were washed at least once weekly. To keep the dogs cool, I provided a kiddie pool for them to play in, as well as ice in their water bowls which were changed frequently. Often, on super-hot days, I also had frozen ice packs made with soda bottles available.

The cats loved the heat of the summer. I had a tin roof, and my father had placed a ladder there as he was working on the roof and windows. The cats discovered it, and Dad was no longer allowed to move the ladder. The cats decided it was there for them. The heat from the tin roof seemed to help the old ones, and they had the opportunity to watch the entire neighborhood.

One thing I learned from my parents is in order to be comfortable in any weather, never create extremes in temperature. For instance, if I want to be able to work outside at noon in 90 degree heat, the worst thing to do is to sit in air conditioning until I'm ready to go out. So, if I want my animals to be comfortable in summer heat, or winter cold, I either could not bring them in a super cool or super warm house. For me, being so animal focused, I made the decision to not use the air conditioning or the heat until absolutely necessary. It also saved tons of money. I did chose to keep the bedroom a little more comfortable so I could sleep. In doing this, I could bring the animals in and out to spend time with me without worrying about the extremes in temperature causing them problems.

So in order to acclimate the animals to the change in seasons, we all experienced the changes together. When the winter did get cold enough to turn the gas heat on, I kept it as low as possible. Those who wanted to wear nice warm sweaters, did, but many didn't want one and would remove it.

One of the best ways to stay warm outside in the winter time, is a dry space and a lose bale of straw. Immediate puppy pile. In fact, the cats loved straw too. I would buy it several times during the winter. Everyone thought it was a wonderful game when new straw was thrown around. Keep in mind that animals that cuddle together stay warmer.

I still needed to provide a several places for the dogs to keep the peace, so I came up with four ideas. I always tried using what I had instead of purchasing. The one essential was straw. I always tried to buy the best. The scrap bales didn't keep them as warm or last as long. On the following page, were the four options I tried.

4 PLANS FOR KEEPING THE ANIMALS WARM

- A "PUPPY PILE BOX" – this was made from some scrap wood we had laying around. Keeping in mind I had on average about 10 dogs, we made a 4 x 4 area on the covered patio that was about 2 ft. high and filled it with warm straw. A diagram is below.

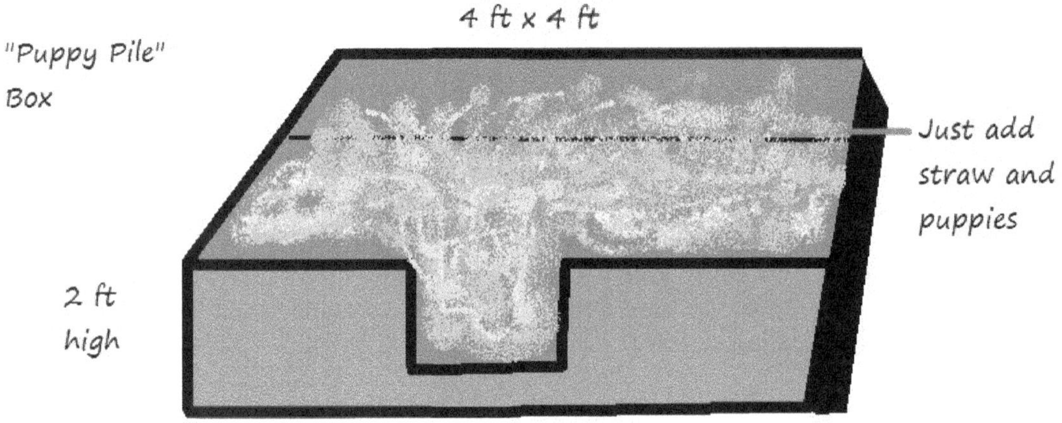

- INSULATE THE DOG KENNELS- The keys to keeping the dog kennels warm in the winter time was to lift them off the ground and insulate them. I used an old toddler bed frame to lift them off the ground. It didn't make it so high that they couldn't jump into their kennels. This way, they were also stacked neatly together. I took old cardboard and wrapped the kennels, then wrapped that in a large tarp using bungee cords to hold it in place. It kept the wind out and the body heat in. I then used straw as bedding. Even the warmest blanket can get frozen and uncomfortable in cold weather. Putting cardboard down on the toddler bed before adding the kennels or adding straw underneath added additional insulation. The diagram is on the following page.

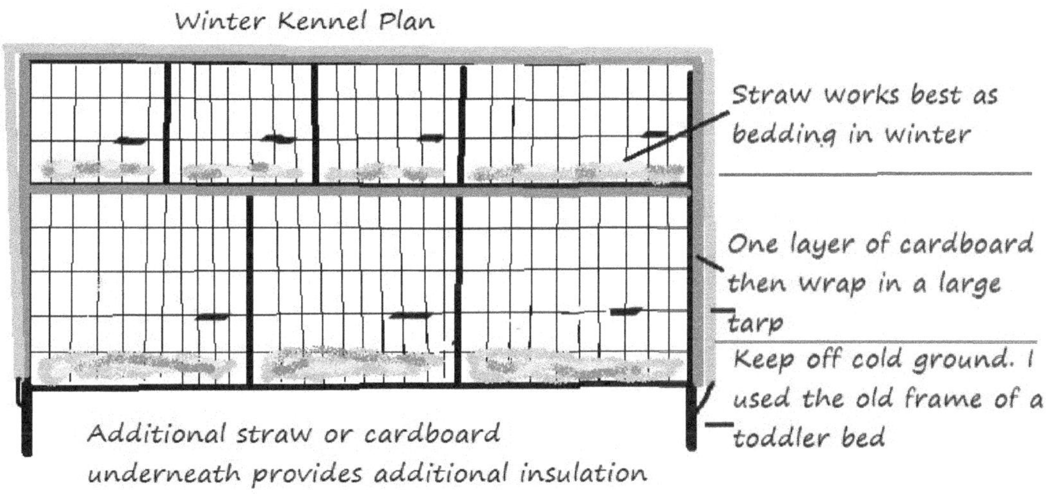

- HEAT THE DOG HOUSE- My dad has always converted our dog houses into heated ones. Drilling a hole in the back near the roof, he fitted a 15 watt bulb and encased it so that the dog nor the bedding would touch it. It's important to position the house so that the electric wire (the part on the outside) will not be reached by the dog. Pushing it up against a fence or building usually does the trick. It is a good idea to put it on a timer so it is only on at night unless you live where it is freezing cold. Here in Tennessee, dogs rarely need it during the day. Another important consideration is not getting a doghouse that is too big for your dog. Remember hot or warm air rises and if the house is too big, the heat will rise to the top of the doghouse and away from your dog. The diagram for that is on the following page. An alternative if you have a large group of dogs (or cats) that get along well is to combine the puppy pile box and the heated dog house. Having them all cuddle together in straw inside a heated dog house is probably the greatest option of all, but make sure one pet doesn't get selfish and keep others outside.

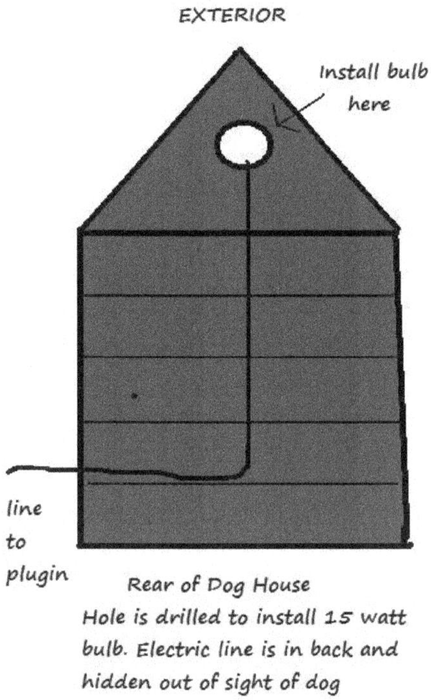

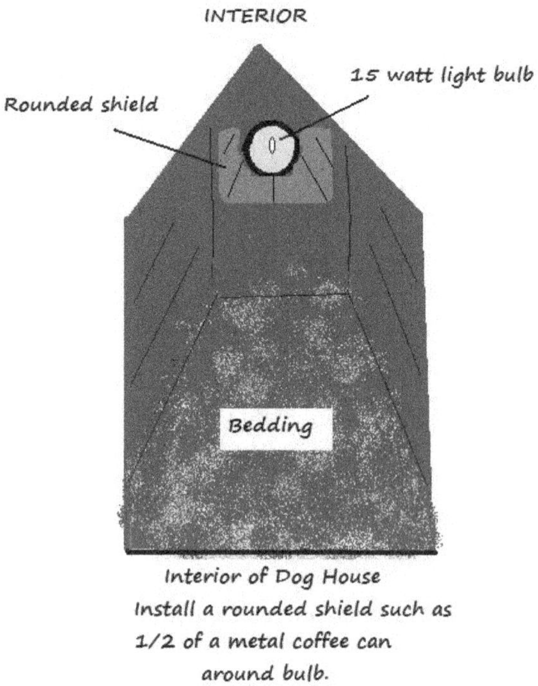

- INSULATE WITH STRAW BALES- straw is a wonderful insulator and it is also a great wind breaker. My father actually had this idea after seeing it done around human homes in areas of cold, high winds, and flat ground. To make it work, surround your dog house on all sides with intact straw bales and cover with a tarp that you stake to the ground. You can also install a cover over the door to keep out of the wind. Cheap ideas for that are small floor mats for cars you can buy at Wal-Mart. If wind primarily blows from one direction, face the door away from the wind, and it will stay much warmer for your pet. A diagram of this idea is on the following page.

ADDITIONAL COST SAVING IDEAS

- Use fallen, dried pine needles for bedding. If you have white pines nearby, rake up the brown needles once they dry. They smell good and feel great too.

- Use hydrated lime as a deodorizer. It may change the pH of your lawn, so check with your local garden center, but it is safe to use. I remove the pets from the area as it is dusty like diatomaceous earth, but then let them back in after the dust has settled.

- If you have a big old dog that needs lots of cushioning, instead of paying top dollar for a dog bed, pay between $10-20 for a toddler mattress at your local thrift store.

- When dog clothing is too expensive, buy kids clothes! Infant to toddler, fits most and at thrift stores are a dime a dozen.

- For inexpensive cat litter, buy Oil Dri ® Premium Absorbant. It is sold in the auto supply and cleaning section at Sams Club. A 40 lb. bag is less than $5. You can always add baking soda to help with odor.

- For most pets, one of the best deterrents to bad behavior is a spray bottle filled with water.

- If you have several cats, sometimes its cheaper making your own litter boxes. I have made large ones using big Rubbermaid Containers and cutting a hole in the side. Keeping the top on makes it look like a storage box, but it is a covered litter box in disguise.

- Vet offices always have an overabundance of Styrofoam ® containers. Medications, vaccines and more are shipped in them weekly. Ask your vet for a couple, cut a hole just big enough for your cat to crawl in, and you have a wonderful cozy bed for your outdoor kitty.

For issues with your pet's water freezing in winter, heated water bowls are available. However, it requires electricity which may not be possible or safe for your situation. Making a well-insulated one isn't very difficult. I combined several different ideas I found on the internet to create the idea below for my pets. The buckets that work best for these are strong rubberized buckets purchased in feed stores. Make sure there is enough room when choosing your buckets for plenty of foam insulation. Depending on the size of your pet, you can make them taller or shorter, or even adjust how deep you bury the buckets accordingly. Make sure the ball you use is big enough that your pet cannot swallow it and that it floats.

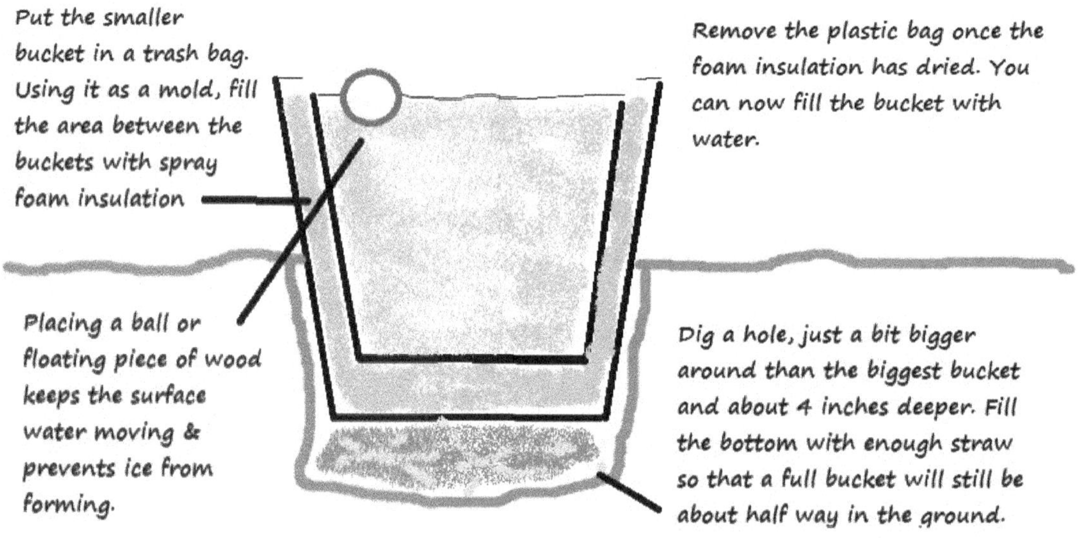

- For coprophagia or the process of eating feces (a nasty dog habit), sprinkle MSG powder on the food of the "poop-E" (not the offender). It is the main ingredient, along with wheat gluten of the product For-bid ®. Normally doing this for about a week will solve the problem.

- If you can't afford puppy pads, newspaper is usually the cheap answer. It allows the urine to go through to your floor which can be an issue. A simple solution is to put either a small plastic tarp or a waterproof plastic baby changing pads underneath the newspaper. While you will need to rinse the waterproof plastic, you won't be spending tons on puppy pads either. However, if you do decide to buy puppy pads, the best buy I have found is Disney's 101 Dalmatian puppy pads for around $20. Its 101 pads. I found mine at Kroger's.

- Instead of buying toys, make them. Just like with kids, you buy an expensive toy only to find out they would prefer a pot and a spatula to beat it with. For my cats, I cut holes in big cardboard boxes and make them a fort. Give them a paper grocery bag. My dogs think nothing is as fun as an empty plastic bottle without the lid. Another thing they love is the cardboard roll left over from paper towels. Instead of buying the expensive toys with no inside stuffing, make a hole, and remove the stuffing from old stuffed animals. Just make sure there are no parts that your pet can swallow, like the eyes and nose. They could care less what their toys look like, they just want to play! Look around at what you have before you buy.

- It is always a good idea to keep your pet's intestinal tract in good shape. Probiotics are the way to do this. An inexpensive and tasty way to do it is yogurt. Most vets recommend plain yogurt, but for a treat, I will occasionally give my dogs blueberry yogurt. Adding it to their food once a week will do wonders for keeping the flora of the intestinal tract in good working order.

- If you feel like you need to buy more expensive food, make it last by adding vegetables such as green beans. You can even mix it with a less expensive food. Remember, just do the best you can.

CHAPTER 14

SMALL ANIMALS, POCKET PETS, BIRDS AND EXOTICS

I have raised, cared for, rescued, and otherwise loved, many types of non-canine and feline pets.

As I mentioned, I had a small animal/pocket pet rescue for a time and as a pet sitter, I took care of everything including snakes, iguanas, chameleons, tortoise, frogs, birds, bunnies, guinea pigs, ferrets, rats, gerbils, and more. My one regret was never working in a vet office that saw lots of these little guys.

As much as I know about them, there is more that I probably don't know, which makes it all the more exciting. I love to learn.

Having taken care of so many in rescue, one thing I do know....it is very helpful if you can grow as much of your own food as possible. It is also important to know the ingredients of each food so you know if it is cheaper to mix your own, or if you get in a tight spot, what can you feed, until you can afford better? That's what this chapter is about.

Some of my methods have been unconventional, and I will not claim they were the very best. However, they were what we had to do to survive.

Probably the easiest way to get started is to tell you about my experience with my birds. For a time, I could barely feed them. I tried several times to re-home them, but Sago, my cockatiel was not friendly at all and so no one wanted him. Thankfully, while writing this book, I found them a good home. However, during that time, this is the story of how I kept them fed.

BIRDS:
Most bird enthusiasts will tell you that for optimum nutrition, your bird should eat commercially prepared pellets along with fresh fruits and vegetables according to bird type. Unless raised on pellets and denied the seeds, most birds will choose seeds. When I was better off financially in California, I had attempted to change my birds from seed to pellets. All I got was plenty of pellets to clean up. So for years, my birds had been eating mostly seed supplemented with fruits and veggies.

The first bird I ever owned, was Zeb. He was a zebra finch. He lived on seeds and fresh fruits and veggies and he always had a cuttlebone for minerals. I did not know at the time that pellets were necessary. Zeb lived a wonderful life and finally passed away at age 10.

So when times got bad, I studied seeds. I took notice of the type of seed in each kind of commercial bird food. Then we compared it to other bird seed bags. I found that many of the same type of ingredients were found in each bag. (See chart below for comparison).

I also looked at wild bird seed for an emergency situation. The problem with some wild bird seed is it can be much higher in fat than domestic bird food. This is to give the birds the energy they need to fly. The cheaper wild bird food also had too much corn and sunflower seeds. So, it was not something we could use on a regular basis. However, if push came to shove, a few days of wild bird food was better than no bird food at all.

I found the best way to stretch my bird see was with wild finch food. A 2lb bag of domestic finch food cost about $6.50 while I could buy a 7.5 lb. bag of wild finch food for around $8.99. It was a huge difference. I combined the finch and cockatiel food together. I realize that bird enthusiast will consider me insane and irresponsible to have my finch and cockatiel together, but it worked for many years.

If you live near a bird farm, it is a wonderful place to get fresh bird seed at an excellent cost. In California I visited Bracken's Bird Farm in Riverside, CA and/or Redlands, CA monthly to purchase in bulk. I had many more birds at the time, and the cost of the seed was affordable thanks to them.

BIRD SEED COMPARISON CHART

ALL NATURAL COCKATIEL FOOD:	WILD FINCH BLEND	ALL NATURAL FINCH BLEND
White Proso Millet, Gray Stripe Sunflower, Oat Groats, Canary Grass Seed, Whole Oats, Safflower, Flaked Corn, Red Proso Millet, Buckwheat, Black Oil Sunflower.	white proso millet, canary grass seed, red proso millet, sunflower chips and thistle seed	White Proso Millet, German Millet, Oat Groats, Red Siberian Millet, Canary Grass Seed, Red Proso Millet.

In Tennessee however, there was no such place I could find. By comparing the type of seed in each food, I was able to figure out what the basics of what they needed at a price I could afford. I am very thankful that they now have a new home where they can get the specific food they need.

One thing to keep in mind is the basics of what your pet needs. It is different with exotics. While your dogs needs dog food and water, birds, for instance, need more. In addition to the seed, birds need grit, cuttle bones, mineral blocks, and a lava block to keep the beak trim and healthy. That's the minimum. You have to make sure you consider all aspects of care.

POCKET PETS:HAMSTERS/GERBILS/MICE/RATS:
If you have several "pocket pets", knowing the basics of what they need and then comparing them to each other can save you a lot of money. Depending on the number of tiny ones you have, it may be cheaper to make your own pocket pet food.

Corn, Oats, Wheat, Milo, Sunflower, Millet, Green Split Peas, Oat Groats, Shelled Peanuts, Ground Wheat, Ground Corn, Sun-cured Alfalfa Meal, Dehulled Soybean Meal, Pumpkin Seed, Barley, Raisins, Dehydrated Carrots, Dried Bananas, Safflower, Canadian Field Peas, Ground Flax Seed, Ground Oats, Dried Papaya, Ground Rice, Dehydrated Sweet Potatoes, Dehydrated Apples, Rice Flour, Dicalcium Phosphate, Calcium Carbonate

HAMSTER AND GERBIL FOOD MAIN INGREDIENTS

Rolled Corn, Rolled Oat Groats, Rolled Barley, Ground Corn, Dehulled Soybean Meal, Wheat Middlings, Ground Wheat, Sun-cured Alfalfa Meal, Meat Meal, Sunflower, Peanuts, Corn Gluten Meal, Cane Molasses, Vegetable Oil, Poultry Meal, Fish Meal, Salt, Beet Pulp, Calcium Carbonate,

MOUSE AND RAT FOOD MAIN INGREDIENTS

For the most part, their needs are very similar. Making a similar-seed mixture and adding fresh fruits or vegetables makes for a healthy pet. The dried "fruits and veggies" found in most brand name mixtures are often created using food coloring, which is not healthy for them.

Both need calcium carbonate. An easy source is eggshells. After making your eggs, bake the eggshells for a few minutes, and let cool. Add a little to their food.

Mice and rats appreciate a bit of meat protein. This is one way their food needs differ from hamsters and gerbils. So I add a little cat food or give them a doggie Milk bone ®

One thing that hamsters and gerbils do need that is not required as much by rats and mice is a salt and mineral wheel. Sometimes, it will seem that they are ignoring the wheel and you will assume they don't need it, but keep in mind how tiny their "licks" are. Leave it in the cage, but if it gets dirty, change it.

It is just as important to know what not to feed these little guys. Never feed potatoes, onions, garlic, citrus, fruit seeds, chocolate or sweets. And remember not to overdo the fresh food or to allow it to spoil. This can cause intestinal problems and even death.

GUINEA PIGS AND RABBITS

The diet of the guinea pig and rabbit is similar, but I have always heard the warning "Do NOT feed guinea pigs rabbit pellets!" The reason for this is two-fold. One, guinea pig food contains vitamin C. Guinea pigs cannot make their own, and they need it in their food. Although not enough on its own to satisfy their needs, it is more than is needed by rabbits. Two, rabbit food can often contain antibiotics in the food which can be toxic to guinea pigs. So, they are correct in saying you should not mix the pellets. My answer is...don't use pellets at all.
Here is the diet comparison of the rabbit and guinea pig:

Sun-cured Timothy Grass Hay, Oat Hulls, Sun-cured Alfalfa Meal, Wheat Middlings, Dehulled Soybean Meal, Dried Cane Molasses, Ground Flax Seed, Salt,

RABBIT FOOD MAIN INGREDIENTS

Sun-cured Alfalfa Meal, Dehulled Soybean Meal, Ground Corn, Rolled Oat Groats, Rolled Barley, Wheat Middlings, Ground Oats, Ground Wheat, Cane Molasses, Soy Oil, Salt,

GUINEA PIG FOOD MAIN INGREDIENTS

What both the rabbit and guinea pig need are a variety of hays, fresh fruit and vegetables, water, and a salt and mineral block.

It is important to understand a little about hay. There is grass hay: timothy, wheat, meadow, orchard, and bermuda and then there is legume hay: alfalfa being the most common. The two often found in stores are timothy and alfalfa. Timothy should be the basis for what you feed both guinea pig and rabbit. While alfalfa is good to mix in occasionally, it is too much of a good thing. Any time you can find fresh orchard grass or any other grass hay, it's a good idea to include those as well. If you live in the country, you can ask local farmers if you could pick up some of what they have left behind after harvesting.

When feeding fresh fruits and vegetables, introduce them slowly and don't overdo it. Remember that guinea pigs HAVE to have vitamin C which is only provided by the food you eat, and no matter what any pellet manufacturer claims, what is in pellets is not enough. I always relied on kale and oranges to supply it for my guinea pigs.

Foods to avoid for both guinea pig and rabbit include: iceberg lettuce, cabbage, cauliflower (both gas producing), shelled seeds and nuts, potato peelings, rhubarb, turnips, raw beans, fruit seeds, dairy, meat, sugary foods, caffeine, breads, processed foods.

Keep in mind, one of the things you can do to save a little money is to grow some of your own vegetables. Kale, green leaf lettuce, green bell peppers, apples and carrots are just a few. If you have an area of the yard that you know has not been treated with pesticides, three of the best and cheapest foods in the world for rabbits and guinea pigs is.....the dandelion, plantain, and clover.

Plantain Weed Clover Weed Dandelion Weed

REPTILES AND AMPHIBIANS

The number of potential pets in this group is astounding. Tortoises are probably my favorite, but living in a more temperate climate and not wanting to keep a tortoise in a tank required me to adopt out my Russian Tortoise before leaving California. As I have said, I have loved and cared for many types of reptiles and amphibians. I have refrained from keeping snakes only at the insistence of family and friends who threaten never to visit again. And while I have fed snakes frozen mice while pet sitting, my love for mice and rats make snake keeping a little more than I wish to deal with.

Most of the pets I have kept have been cricket, mealworm, earthworm, or feeder fish connoisseurs. So those are the things I learned to grow. While buying them in bulk online can be a very smart move, sometimes, paying practically nothing (after a while) is even better. Here are some ideas for growing your own feeders at home.

HOW TO RAISE CRICKETS

- Get an old aquarium or a deep plastic container. You will need a mesh lid or some way to keep them inside. Be sure they get plenty of ventilation.

- Fill the bottom with play sand about an inch deep or nothing at all. There are advantages and disadvantages for both.

- One one side of the container place a separate plastic container (about 4 in x 4 in) with soil. Do not use soil sold at garden shops because it often contains pesticides. A good alternative is soil sold for reptile tanks. Once the soil is in the small container, fill that container about half full with water. This soil must stay moist, but do not allow it to mold. This is your breeding chamber.

- Put several egg crates inside. This is to make sure that the crickets are not crowded. These can be purchased at Tractor Supply in the poultry section. Old toilet paper rolls work too, but in my experience not as well.

- You can make your own food, but I find it much easier and cost effective to use something like Flunker's High Calcium Cricket Food. That way I'm sure they are getting the right nutrition. For water, use a potato slice or orange slice, but be sure they do not spoil. Flunker's also has a gel that provides moisture without drowning the crickets and it adds additional moisture.

- The crickets will need to stay warm. Usually around 85 degrees. This can be accomplished with a heating pad set to low or heat lamps. Be careful not to get too hot or too cold.

- Purchase about 30-50 medium to large crickets from the pet store. Once the female has a long stem coming from the abdomen and the male is chirping, breeding has begun.

- Continue to keep the breeding chamber moist. Once eggs are laid, you will see tiny white specks in just under the top layer of the soil. Once you are sure there are several, remove the chamber to another deep plastic container to start the cycle over again.

- Continue to alternate containers and you will have a continuous supply. Expect to wait about a month to two months to have enough of a supply to be able to feed to your critter.

HOW TO RAISE MEAL WORMS

- Purchase one 6 quart plastic container and three 4 quart containers. Each container is for a certain part of the life cycle of the meal worm. (Egg, larvae/worm, pupa, beetle)

- In your 6 qtr. container (container #1) add oats, cornmeal, or wheat bran (about 2-3 inches). This is the bedding and also what the meal worms will eat. Also add a piece of potato or carrot for moisture.

- Purchase at least 100 meal worms (300-500 is ideal) . Avoid giant and super worms.

- Put your meal worms in the 6 qtr. container. If using a lid, make sure they have some ventilation, but not too much to avoid escape. Replace potato or carrot as needed and do not let them spoil.

- Put the container somewhere warm. I put mine on top of my refrigerator.

- As the meal worms mutate to the pupa stage, they will look really strange and curl around in a "C" shape. If you touch them they move. You will need to remove them and put them in container #2 (one of the 4 qtr. containers). I number my containers to make it easier. This container should also have the same oat/bran bedding and a carrot/potato, but only about 1 inch of bedding and a small carrot as they do not eat much during this stage.

- The pupa will again mutate to beetles. Once this occurs, I move them to container #3. You have to check daily as the beetles will eat your pupa. In container #3, also add about the same amount of bedding, but add a bigger carrot/potato. Remember to make sure the veggies are fresh.

- Any beetle that seems unhealthy, discard. It is important to keep the healthiest since their offspring will be providing nutrition for your pet.

- Once about 10-20 healthy beetles are doing well, it is time to separate the bedding (which contains the eggs) from the beetles, as they will eat the eggs. The easiest way to separate them is to put an apple slice inside. The beetles will grab the apple and you can simply remove the apple.

- Using your #4 container, put the apple and the beetles inside temporarily. Take the bedding from the #3 container and put it in the #1 container. This eggs will hatch and the cycle will begin again.

- Put new bedding in container #3 for the beetles to allow them to lay more eggs.

- When the bedding has become too dirty to use (3-6 months, put the old bedding in another container in case there are more eggs to hatch, and add new bedding to your containers.

HOW TO RAISE FEEDER GUPPIES:

Feeder guppies are not the fancy guppies you see sold in stores. They are smaller and the males have light rainbow colors. The females are plain in color. I have never seen a more prolific fish. One female can produce 40-60 fry at one time. Here is how to do it:

- Depending on how many you need, start with two tanks. I suggest a 5-10 gallon for the adults and a 2.5-5 gallon for the fry (baby fish). Set up the tank before purchasing the fish. Make sure the water is de-chlorinated and at an appropriate tropical fish temperature. Take care of these guys just as good as you would a pet fish. Not only do they deserve it, but it makes for healthier food for your frogs.

- Purchase about 2 dozen adult feeder guppies. Make sure there are not a lot of dead fish floating in the tank. If so, wait until next time or go to another store. As the pet store employee for as many pregnant females as they can find. The darker and bigger the spot near their vent on their tummy, the more likely the female is pregnant.

- Put the adults in the tank. If you have any females that look like they may give birth soon, be prepared to move them to the smaller tank for delivery.

- Your smaller fry tank needs to be densely planted. Give the fry plenty of places to hide. Keep in mind, you may not be present when mom gives birth, and she will eat them if given half a chance.

- As soon as she gives birth, move her back to the adult tank. Once the fry are big enough, they can join the adults and the cycle can continue.

There are other food items you can raise for your frogs and other pets: mosquito larvae, brine shrimp, and even blood worms. They all have their own level of difficulty and expense. The cheapest and easiest is the mosquito larvae. You have to be particularly careful with mosquito larvae to ensure that they don't become mosquitoes. Mosquitoes spread disease, not only for people, but for pets. I have to be careful to check my dogs' and cats' water bowls frequently, dump them, and freshen them to prevent the eggs from hatching.

HOW TO RAISE MOSQUITO LARVAE:

- Using a small bucket, fill it with water. I start with warm water.

- Sit the bucket in the sun. The water will start to turn green. This is good. The green is an algae.

- Check the bucket daily. You should start seeing tiny clusters of dark brown eggs. These should be about the size of a sesame seed or tiny grain of brown rice.

- You can put these eggs in the tank and allow your frog to eat the larvae as they hatch, (if they will wait). If feeding them to your feeder guppies (also known as mosquito fish!), you can go ahead and put the eggs inside.

- Using a brine shrimp net, which is smaller than a fish net, you can net the wigglers once they hatch. I carry a cup outside with me, scoop some of their water in it, net the wigglers, and put them in the cup for transport. I then net them again to transfer to the fish or frog tank.

- Make sure that the wigglers do not mature to adult mosquitoes. If you have to dump your bucket and start over because you have too many, do it. Or better yet, isolate them to a small ice cube tray (the one for tiny ice cubes) and freeze them so you will have some for winter.

COST SAVING TIPS FOR YOUR SMALL ANIMALS & EXOTICS:

- Don't assume that the only source of supplies for your pet is in the reptile aisle. For instance, instead of paying $10 for dried meal worms to treat your pet, spend $5 and buy Happy Hen ® Mealworm Frenzy for chickens. It's found in the chicken department at feed stores.

- If needing just a heat lamp for your pet, incandescent lights are cheaper. Black lights sold as party lights work at night, but be sure you are using the proper UVA/UVB lights as well.

- If your UVA/UVB light goes out in the summer before your paycheck comes, take your pet outside for an hour or so. Be sure to use all precautions to make sure he/she is safe, cannot escape and is not easily overheated. NEVER leave your lizard in the sun alone.

- Learn to think outside the box. If you have no other pets and want your guinea pig to have more room, get a large kiddie pool and fill with bedding.

- Cardboard makes a bored rat very happy. Mine have made homes out of cereal boxes and then torn them apart for fun. A little mess is okay. The same goes for bunnies. They love to tear up phone books. Ask friends for their old ones.

- If your rabbit is outside in the summer, she will enjoy sitting on a frozen water filled soda bottle.

- If you know your grass has not been treated with pesticides, take the top of your guinea pig cage and your guinea pig, and let them graze for a while. Make sure to stay with them and put them in an area where no dogs or cats have defecated.

- Buy pine or aspen bedding in bulk. It is much cheaper and you can always keep the extra in a container until it is needed.

- Rake up pine needles for bedding. Although I was concerned about this method at first, I have never had a problem with using it for my guinea pigs.

CHAPTER 15

AND THE WORK CONTINUES

As much as I have learned over the years, I am still struggling to keep us all together. We are poor in finances. Yet, in love, our family is rich beyond imagination.

Sometimes hard decisions have to be made for the good of the pets. As I was writing this book, I had many I had to make. I had to decide, for instance, who needs ME and who is happy just being taken care of? So I found homes for the birds and frogs. I had to decide that my little guinea pig, Polly, who was nearly 7 years old, needed to be euthanized because her quality of life was no longer good. I had to decide to sell things that were important to me to make ends meet. But those things were only things, not my fur-kids.

It is all about discovering what is important to you, and what you can sacrifice. I gave up television and home phone, for instance. I'm very conscious of how much electricity, natural gas, and water I use. I think of ways to utilize what I have before I think of buying something else. It's all about prioritizing your life.

Even though I have given up material things for my little guys, not for one minute do I think I have suffered. When I look at my animals and see that those who were broken by fear and sadness return that gaze with peace and happiness, I am blessed. When I find myself crying from all the stress only to look up and find myself surrounded by my cats, I am honored. In the quiet and loneliness of life, my big robust family keeps me company.

And perhaps my methods are not the absolute "best practice" you would find in professional veterinary books. I'm sure even many pet enthusiasts would say I was a horrid pet parent. However, these are the things I did to take care of my family and I stand by them.

I have found that material things are unimportant to me. I need only the bare necessities of life. It is the soul and spirit of the animals in my care that bring me joy. I have in my 40+ years realized that life is enjoyed in a heart that is loved, not in the money that is spent.

Although my pockets may remain empty, and my wallet may remain small, my big heart will keep beating and I will continue to share all that I have with all the little critters that come my way. And in doing so, I will find my own hidden treasure in the peace that comes from being loved by all those tiny hearts.

APPENDIX & LINKS FOR ADDITIONAL INFORMATION

VETERINARY MANUALS

- Merck Veterinary Manual www.merckvetmanual.com
- Veterinary Formulary www.ahc.umn.edu/rar/umnuser/formulary.html

VACCINE IMMUNITY & PROTOCOLS

- Duration of Immunity to Canine Vaccines www.cedarbayvet.com/duration_of_immunity.htm
- Long Term Immunity of Cat Vaccines www.ncbi.nlm.nih.gov/pubmed/10328440
- 2003 Report of AAHA Canine Vaccine Task Force www.terrierman.com/AAHA-Vaccine-Report.pdf
- Vaccinations for Immunocompromised Pets- http://devinefarm.net/rp/rpvaccin.htm
- Canine Immune System & Disease Resistance- www.canine-epilepsy-guardian angels.com/ImmuneSystem.htm

PET FOOD AND NUTRITION

- Evolutionary Basis for Feeding Behavior- http://jn.nutrition.org/content/136/7/1927S.long
- Dry Cat Food Nutritional Information http://binkyspage.tripod.com/dryfood.html
- Wet Cat Food Nutritional Information http://binkyspage.tripod.com/CanFoodNew.html
- Bearded Dragon Nutritional Information http://www.beautifuldragons.com/Nutrition.html
- FDA Pet Food Guidelines- http://www.fda.gov/animalveterinary/products/animalfoodfeeds/petfood/default.htm
- Dog Food Analysis http://dogfoodanalysis.com/
- Consumer Reports Review of Pet Food http://www.consumerreports.org/cro/magazine-archive/2011/august/money/pet-costs/dont-pay-a-premium-for-premium-pet-food/index.htm
- Consumer Reports on Pet Food Prices http://www.consumerreports.org/cro/magazine-archive/march-2009/money/pet-food/overview/pet-food-ov.htm
- Making homemade cat food http://www.catnutrition.org/recipes.html
- Pet Nutritional requirements http://www.eu.elsevierhealth.com/media/us/samplechapters/9780750688079/9780750688079.pdf

LAB WORK

- Images and microscopic views of Intestinal Parasites http://www.pet-informed-veterinary-advice-online.com/fecal-float.html

- Views of blood cells/ringworm/mites www.catnmore.com/animals/microgallery.htm
- Understanding your lab results http://labtestsonline.org/understanding/
- Heart worm Testing http://www.marvistavet.com/html/body_diagnosis_of_heartworm_disease.html

MEDICATIONS AND THEIR DOSAGES

- Veterinary Formulary http://www.ahc.umn.edu/rar/umnuser/formulary.html
- 1800PetMeds-dosages for all pet medication http://www.1800petmeds.com/
- Pet Only Pharmacy http://www.pet-scripts.com/
- Generic & Discount Pet Meds http://www.joespetmeds.com/

PET HEALTH TOPICS

- Common Pet Medical Issues http://www.petmd.com/
- Wound Dressing and Bandages http://www.eu.elsevierhealth.com/media/us/samplechapters/9780750688079/9780750688079.pdf

FLUID THERAPY

- Instructions for dogs http://www.vetmed.wsu.edu/cliented/dog_fluids.aspx
- Fluids/Fluid Therapy in Reptiles http://www.anapsid.org/fluids.html

ONLINE LINKS WHERE I BUY SUPPLIES

- Nonprescription antibiotics & praziquantel http://www.countrysidepet.com/
- Canine Aspirin & Vaccines http://www.drsfostersmith.com/
- Sub-Q fluids and supplies http://www.atlanticmedsupply.com/
- Dewormers, etc. http://www.tractorsupply.com/

BOOKS FOR RECOMMENDED READING

- Dog Owner's Home Veterinary Handbook, Fourth Edition (Eldredge, Carlson, Giffin, Adelman)
- Cat Owner's Home Veterinary Handbook, Third Edition (Eldredge, Carlson, Giffin, Adelman)
- The Merck/Merial Manual for Pet Health: The complete pet health resource for your dog, cat, horse or other pets - in everyday language. (Merck/Merial, Cynthia Kahn Editor)
- The Bird Care Book (Gerstenfeld)
- Small Animals Question and Answer Manual (Alderton)
- The Exotic Pet Survival Manual (Alderton)
- Pills For Pets: The A to Z Guide to Drugs and Medications for Your Animal Companion (Eldredge)

ABOUT THE AUTHOR

J.C. Farris earned her Bachelors of Arts in Psychology at Carson-Newman College. Finding she was better with animals and their people, she has spent most of her adult life in the animal care field. She completed further vet tech training at Cedar Valley College in Dallas, TX.

She now lives in East Tennessee with her pack of fur-kids and Charlie, the Bearded Dragon. In addition to writing about pet care, she writes a spiritual blog called Whisper Creek. She also writes about her struggles with social agoraphobia and panic disorder. She is working on her next book and continues to rescue.

To reach her, email her at whispercreektales@gmail.com.